Illustrator:
Karon Walstad

Editor:
Janet Cain, M. Ed.

Editorial Project Manager:
Ina Massler Levin, M.A.

Editor-in-Chief:
Sharon Coan, M.S. Ed.

Art Director:
Elayne Roberts

Cover Artist:
Larry Bauer

Production Manager:
Phil Garcia

Imaging:
Hillary Merriman

Publishers:
Rachelle Cracchiolo, M.S. Ed.
Mary Dupuy Smith, M.S. Ed.

May Monthly Activities

Early Childhood

Author:

Dona Herweck Rice

Teacher Created Materials, Inc.
P.O. Box 1040
Huntington Beach, CA 92647
©*1995 Teacher Created Materials, Inc.*
Made in U.S.A.
ISBN-1-55734-868-5

The classroom teacher may reproduce copies of materials in this book for classroom use only. The reproduction of any part for an entire school or school system is strictly prohibited. No part of this publication may be transmitted, stored, or recorded in any form without written permission from the publisher.

Table of Contents

May Calendar 3	**Caterpillars and Butterflies** 43
Parent Request Letter 4	Lesson-Planning Sheet 43
	Parent Sign In/Out Sheet 44
May Day 5	Activities for Home 45
Lesson-Planning Sheet 5	Thematic Activities 46
Parent Sign In/Out Sheet 6	Just for Fun 55
Activities for Home 7	Poem 56
Thematic Activities 8	Stationery 57
Just for Fun 17	Clip Art and Patterns 58
Poem 18	Bookmarks and Badges 60
Stationery 19	Achievement Award 61
Clip Art and Patterns 20	**Trains** 62
Bookmarks and Badges 22	Lesson-Planning Sheet 62
Achievement Award 23	Parent Sign In/Out Sheet 63
Mother's Day 24	Activities for Home 64
Lesson-Planning Sheet 24	Thematic Activities 65
Parent Sign In/Out Sheet 25	Just for Fun 74
Activities for Home 26	Poem 75
Thematic Activities 27	Stationery 76
Just for Fun 36	Clip Art and Patterns 77
Poem 37	Bookmarks and Badges 79
Stationery 38	Achievement Award 80
Clip Art and Patterns 39	
Bookmarks and Badges 41	
Achievement Award 42	

Introduction

The monthly activity books in this series have been created specifically for early childhood students. Every book is divided into four themes, roughly one theme per week of the month. Within each weekly theme there is a lesson-planning sheet; a parent sign in/out sheet; a list of suggested home activities; a number of thematic activities, such as arts and crafts, stories, letters, numbers, colors, shapes, music, movement, and food; a just-for-fun page; an original poem; stationery; clip art and patterns; bookmarks and badges for rewards; and an award certificate for one area of achievement. A calendar pattern, to which each student can add dates and a picture, and a request letter are included for the entire month. The themes for the month of May are *May Day, Mother's Day, Caterpillars and Butterflies,* and *Trains.* A variety of management materials have been included to support each theme, creating a unifying whole. All activities are designed to enhance motor and/or cognitive skills while students are having fun. Most importantly, the activities have been classroom tested — with excellent results.

Use some or all of the pages to support the already exciting early childhood experiences taking place in your classroom.

May Calendar

Sunday	Monday	Tuesday	Wednesday	Thursday	Friday	Saturday

Parent Request Letter

Dear Parents and Guardians,

As you can see by the art on this page, our themes for the upcoming month are *May Day, Mother's Day, Caterpillars and Butterflies,* and *Trains.* We will be completing a variety of projects in order to enhance our fine motor skills, while learning a variety of other skills such as cooperation, following directions, using the imagination, counting, and recognizing letters, colors, and shapes.

In order to complete our projects, we would appreciate any of the following materials that you can send. Thank you in advance!

_____

_____

_____

_____

_____

_____

Best wishes,

_____

May Day   Lesson-Planning Sheet

Activity (circle time, playtime, etc.)	Monday	Tuesday	Wednesday	Thursday	Friday

May Day · Daily Attendance

Parent Sign In/Out Sheet

Parents: Please sign your child in and out under the current date.

Name	Time	Date:	Date:	Date:	Date:	Date:
	In					
	Out					
	In					
	Out					
	In					
	Out					
	In					
	Out					
	In					
	Out					
	In					
	Out					
	In					
	Out					
	In					
	Out					
	In					
	Out					
	In					
	Out					

May Day   Home Activities

May Day Activities for Home

Dear Parents and Guardians,

Our theme of the week is *May Day*. Below is a list of enjoyable activities that you can do with your child. Please support your child's learning by using these activities or by creating some of your own. Your help is greatly appreciated.

Suggested Activities:

- Imagine together that you are flowers. Discuss the things that you might experience throughout the day, such as the sunlight shining on you, a butterfly landing on your petals, or a bee drinking your nectar.

- Take your child to the public library. Check out a storybook or nonfiction book about a flower. Read it together. Discuss your favorite parts.

- Draw and color pictures of flower gardens. Tell about your pictures.

- Work together to make May Day baskets and leave them on the porches of friends or relatives. Ring the doorbell, hide, and watch each person's surprised response to your gift. (Baskets can easily be made from plastic strawberry cartons. Weave colored ribbons through the holes and tie on a yarn handle. Fill the baskets with small, live flowers or flowers made of paper.)

- Tell your child an imaginary story about a flower family that lives in your backyard or at a park.

- Together, watch the flower garden scene from Walt Disney's *Alice in Wonderland* (1951). Discuss the behavior of the flowers.

- Walk through your neighborhood, noticing the flowers on the way. Go to a nursery or flower shop and learn about flowers.

- Make a wreath of real or artificial flowers.

- Read "It's May Day!" with your child. Practice saying it together with lots of expression.

Best wishes,

_____

May Day   *Thematic Activities*

May Day Arts and Crafts I

Create a classroom window box to celebrate May Day. Follow these directions:

Materials:

- cardboard or wooden box, approximately 3' long x 6" wide x 6" high (90 cm x 15 cm x 15 cm)
- aluminum foil
- paint (any color)
- paintbrushes
- plaster of Paris
- green chenille sticks
- construction paper, various colors
- scissors
- glue
- old shirts or smocks (1 per student)

Directions:

1. Inform parents ahead of time of the date for this project since it will be a messy day. You can send parents a note on the May Day stationery (page 19), asking them to send old shirts or smocks if you do not already have some.

2. If a box is not available, make one from pieces of wood or cardboard. Nail, glue, or tape the pieces together.

3. As a class, work together to paint the exterior of the box.

4. While the box is drying, give each student two or three chenille sticks and pieces of construction paper. Have them cut out two leaves and a flower for each chenille stick. Ask students to glue the pieces together to make flowers for the window box.

5. Completely line the interior of the box with aluminum foil.

6. Mix the plaster of Paris. Pour plaster in the box until it is three-quarters full. Let it set long enough to harden slightly but still remain soft enough to allow the chenille sticks to be inserted.

7. Let students insert their flowers into the plaster of Paris. Place your flower box on a shelf near a window and invite students to enjoy the view.

Variation: Give each student a small clay pot. Follow the directions described above, allowing each student to create a flower pot of his or her own instead of making one flower box for the classroom.

May Day *Thematic Activities*

May Day Arts and Crafts II

Students will enjoy becoming flowers by wearing easy-to-make flower hats.

Materials:

- scissors
- flower pattern (shown below)
- glue
- leaf pattern (shown below)
- stapler
- construction paper: green and a variety of other colors

Directions:

1. Cut a headband for each student from green construction paper. Make each headband about 1.5" (4 cm) wide and as long as necessary to fit around the student's head.

2. Help each student use green construction paper to make three copies of the leaf pattern shown below, as well as three stems. Then have students use different colors of construction paper and the pattern shown below to make three flowers.

3. Have students glue the stems, leaves, and flowers to their headbands. Let the glue dry.

4. Staple each headband closed to fit the size of each student's head. If the stems tend to fall over, glue or tape toothpicks to the backs. Have students wear the headbands while moving like flowers (page 16).

©1995 Teacher Created Materials, Inc.   9   #868 May Monthly Activities—Early Childhood

May Day   *Thematic Activities*

May Day Story

As a class, read Jerry Pallotta's *The Flower Alphabet Book* (Charlesbridge Publishing, 1988). You may wish to abridge the text, since it may be too cumbersome for young learners. Discuss with students that there are even more types of flowers than are described in this book.

Ask students to use their imaginations to create flowers of their own. Ask them to describe their flowers, including the colors. Give each student a copy of the frame shown below. Have students draw and color their flowers. Write in the names they give their flowers. Staple their pages together with a cover page that reads "Our Class Flower Book."

My flower is called _____.

May Day   *Thematic Activities*

May Day Letters

Practice the letter **F** for *flower*. Have students color in these giant F's. Ask them if they can make the F's look like the stems of flowers. To do so, they can add lines and details of their own.

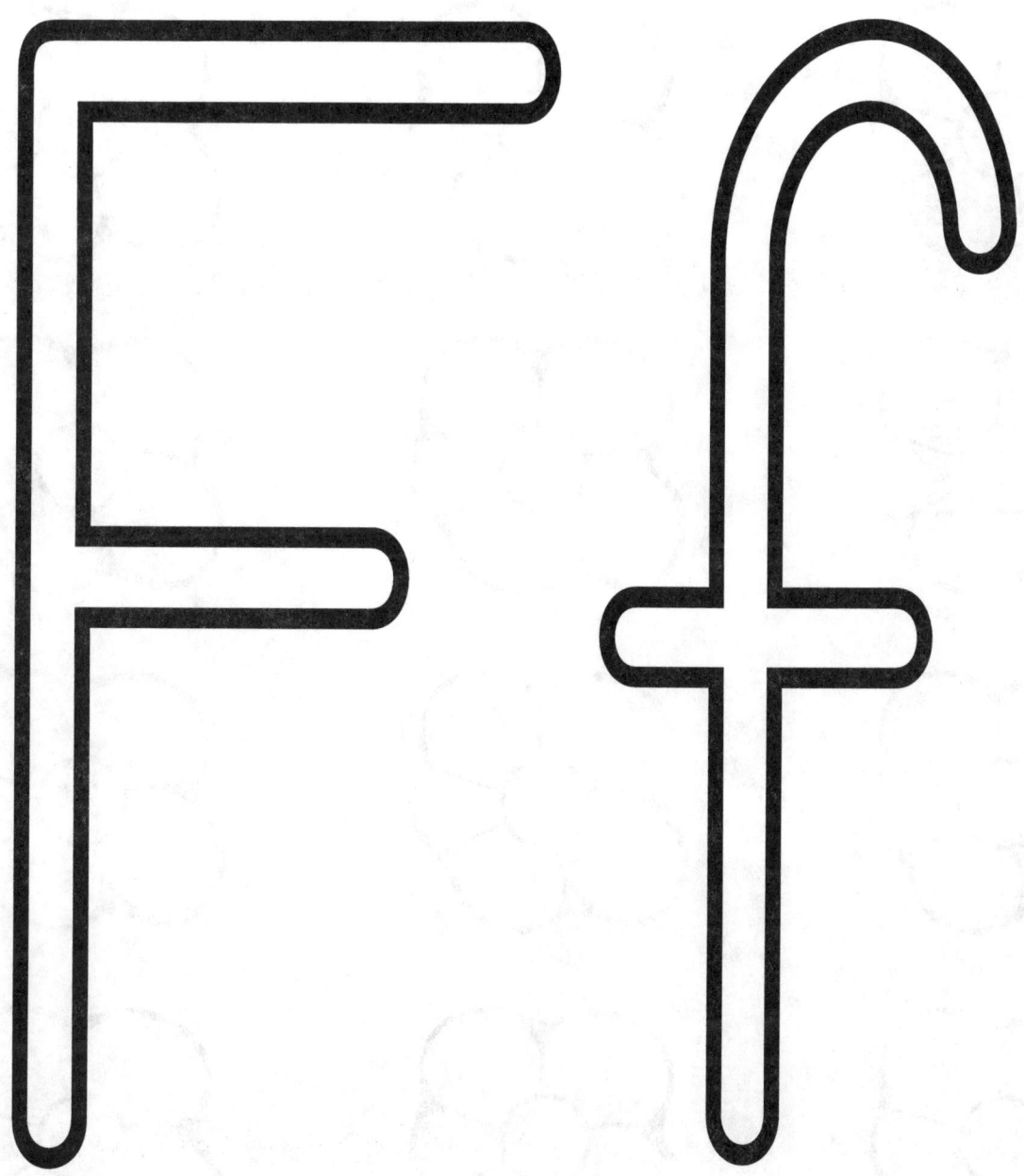

A reward badge for this activity can be found on page 22.

©1995 Teacher Created Materials, Inc.   11   #868 May Monthly Activities—Early Childhood

May Day   *Thematic Activities*

May Day Numbers

Collect small plastic baskets such as those in which strawberries are sold. Duplicate the flowers below and let each student color and cut out a set. Give each student a basket and, together, practice counting. To do so, tell students a number and have them count that number of flowers into the basket. Have students remove the flowers from their baskets and count again.

You may also wish to have students leave the flowers in the basket, add a few more flowers, and then count to find out how many flowers there are all together in the basket.

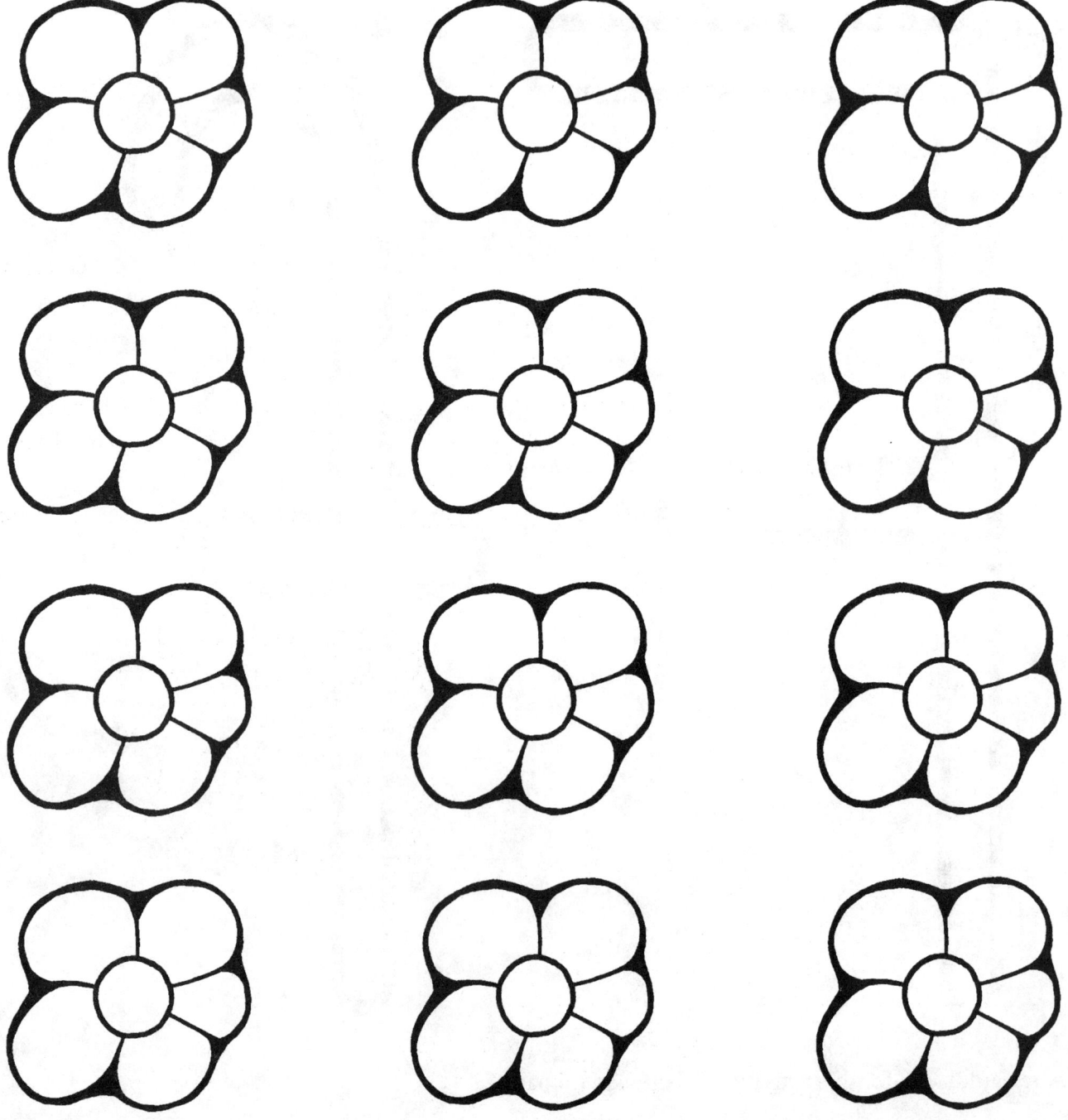

#868 May Monthly Activities—Early Childhood   12   ©1995 Teacher Created Materials, Inc.

May Day   *Thematic Activities*

May Day Colors

Students will enjoy learning about the colors pink and green, using the activity described below.

Materials:

- pink tempera paint, premixed
- paintbrushes (1 per student)
- paper plates or bowls
- large squares of butcher paper
- old shirts or smocks (1 per student)
- newspapers
- green crayons

Directions:

1. Inform parents ahead of time of the date for this project since it will be a messy day. You can send parents a note on the May Day stationery (page 19), asking them to send old shirts or smocks if you do not already have some.

2. Cover the floor with newspapers.

3. Have each student take off his or her shoes and socks, roll up any long pantlegs, and put on smocks. Give each student some pink paint on a paper plate or in a bowl. Also give each student a square of butcher paper. Lay the pieces of butcher paper on top of the newspapers, allowing plenty of work space for each student. Tell students to watch where they step since they will be working on the floor.

4. Show students how to dip the paintbrush into the paint, hold the brush low, and splatter the paint onto the butcher paper. Be sure students understand that they must work carefully so they do not splatter paint on each other, the walls, or objects in the classroom.

5. Allow the paint to dry. Give students green crayons and have them add stems and leaves to these paint-drop flowers.

6. Display the flower paintings around the classroom.

©1995 Teacher Created Materials, Inc.   13   #868 May Monthly Activities—Early Childhood

May Day   *Thematic Activities*

May Day Shapes

Duplicate the patterns below and on page 15 onto heavy paper, one set per student. Let students color their flowers. Then, have them color each of the smaller circles on the large circle using different colors. Cut out the flower and the large circle. Then, cut out the circle in the center of the flower. Attach the large circle behind the flower. Use a brad to attach them at the black dots. Spin the circle so that the differently colored small circles appear in the center of the flower.

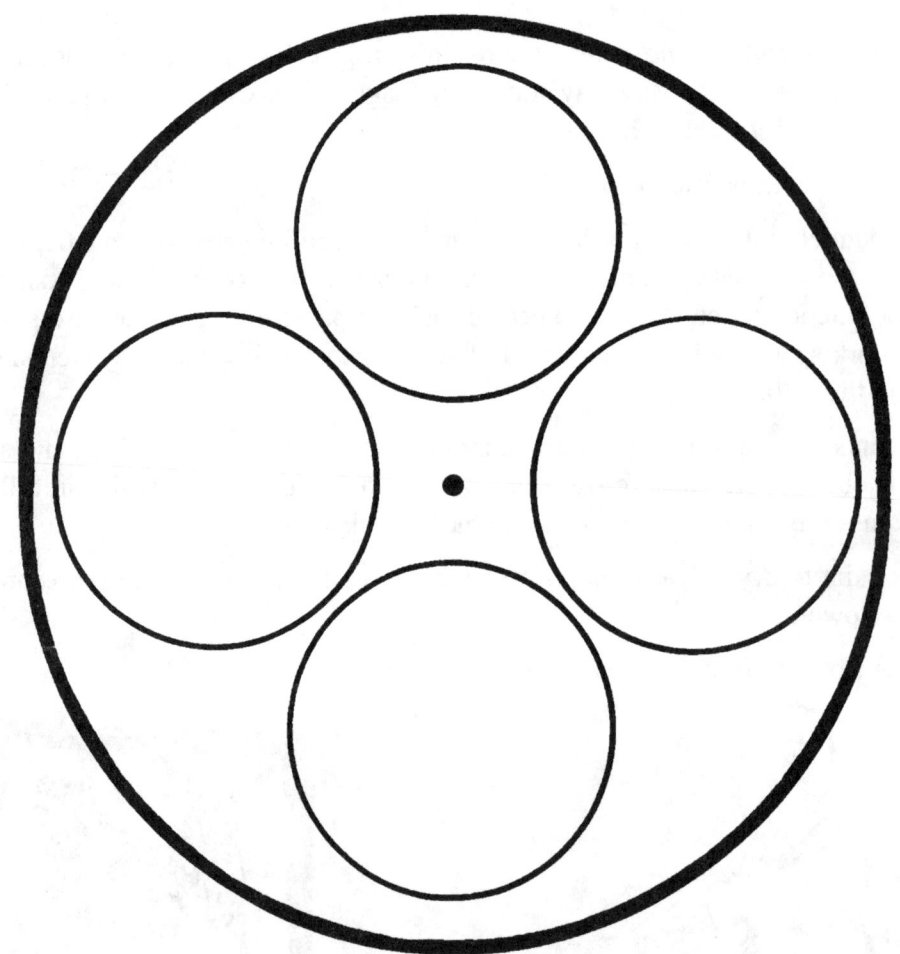

May Day   *Thematic Activities*

May Day Shapes (cont.)

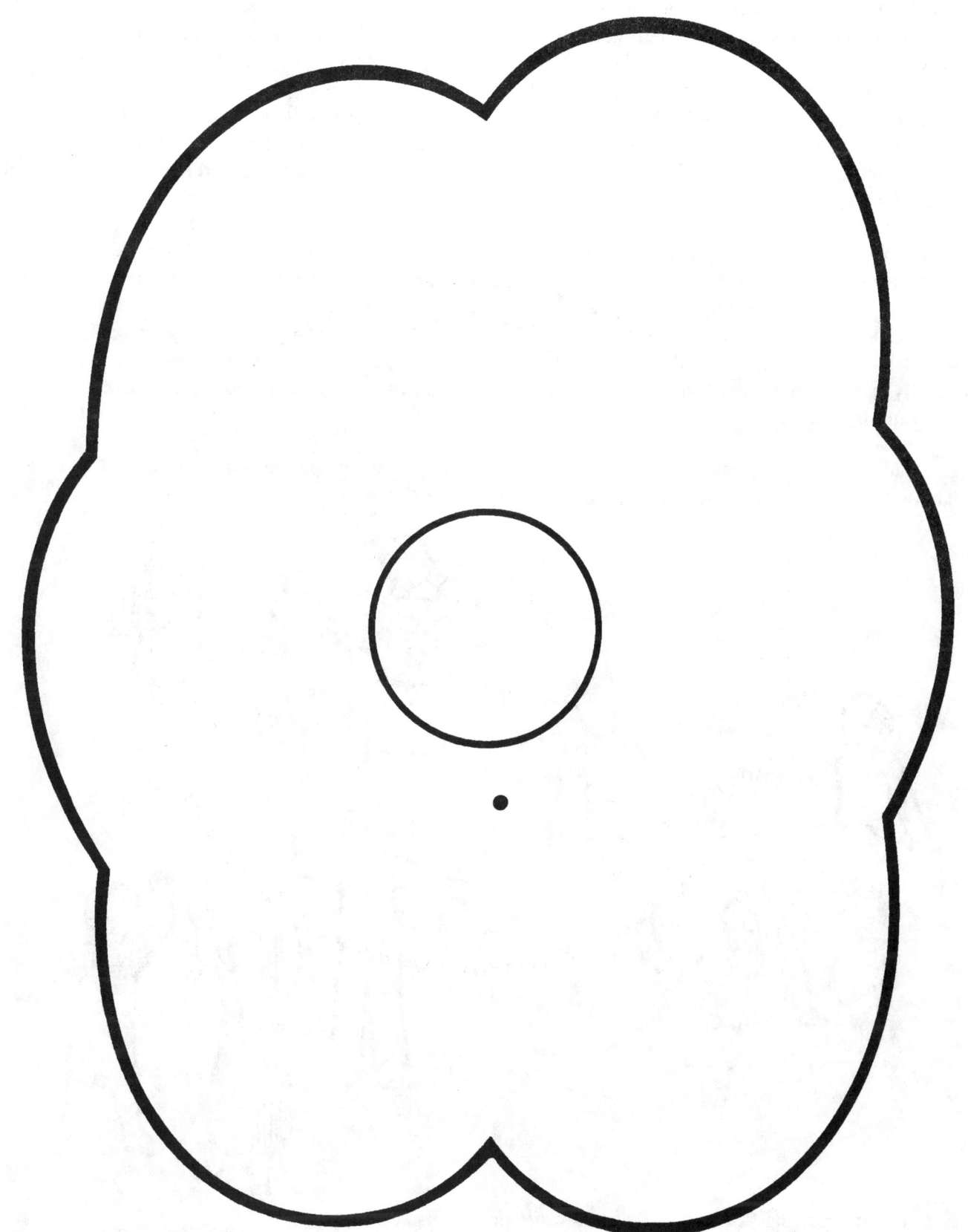

May Day   *Thematic Activities*

May Day Movements

Children love pantomime and certainly have the imaginations to portray anything they desire. Foster their imaginations and nurture their motility by leading them to become a garden of flowers. Here is how.

First, explain to students the basic process by which a seed becomes a flower. The seed lies in the ground and is touched by the warmth of the sun. It begins to shoot down roots into the ground and to push a stem up into the air. The stem grows leaves. At the top of the stem, a bud appears and blossoms into a flower.

Next, tell students that they are going to pretend to be a garden of flowers. Turn off the lights and have students curl up in balls on the floor. Tell them to imagine that they are the seeds. Turn on the lights. Explain that this is the sunlight. Have students extend their legs and wriggle their toes to show that their roots are growing. Ask them to stand. Tell students that this means their stems are pushing out into the sun. They can then extend their arms for leaves, wriggling their fingers as they do this. Finally, have students shake their heads as their flowers unfold. Then, the whole flower can gently sway in the breeze.

Let students repeat the activity. You may wish to challenge their cognitive and physical skills by having them work backwards through the steps described above.

Extension: Wear the flower hats (page 9) while doing this activity.

#868 *May Monthly Activities—Early Childhood*   16   ©1995 Teacher Created Materials, Inc.

May Day   Just for Fun

May Day Maze

Deliver the May basket to the house by following the maze.

©1995 Teacher Created Materials, Inc.   17   #868 May Monthly Activities—Early Childhood

It's May Day!

It's May Day! It's May Day!
May Day is here!
The flowers are blooming,
It's spring, my dear!

Come see the flowers,
Come hear the bees,
Spread out a picnic
Under the trees.

It's May Day! It's May Day!
May Day is here!
It's time to be happy,
Time for good cheer!

May Day   *Patterns*

Clip Art and Patterns

May Day *Patterns*

Clip Art and Patterns *(cont.)*

©1995 Teacher Created Materials, Inc. #868 May Monthly Activities—Early Childhood

May Day — Rewards

Bookmarks and Badges

Have students color the crayons pink and green and wear the badges home.

Have students color their badges and wear them home.

Have students choose their favorite flowers and then color their badges. They can wear the badges home.

Although most early childhood students have not yet learned to read, they enjoy having bookmarks to use while reading with their families at home.

#868 May Monthly Activities—Early Childhood ©1995 Teacher Created Materials, Inc.

May Day *Award*

Achievement Award

has earned our

Classroom Achievement Award

for excellent

COOPERATION!

_____ Date

_____ Teacher's Signature

Mother's Day   Lesson-Planning Sheet

Activity (circle time, playtime, etc.)	Monday	Tuesday	Wednesday	Thursday	Friday

Mother's Day   *Daily Attendance*

Parent Sign In/Out Sheet

Parents: Please sign your child in and out under the current date.

Name	Time	Date:	Date:	Date:	Date:	Date:
	In					
	Out					
	In					
	Out					
	In					
	Out					
	In					
	Out					
	In					
	Out					
	In					
	Out					
	In					
	Out					
	In					
	Out					
	In					
	Out					
	In					
	Out					

©1995 Teacher Created Materials, Inc.   #868 May Monthly Activities—Early Childhood

Mother's Day — Home Activities

Mother's Day Activities for Home

Dear Parents and Guardians,

This week we will be learning about *Mother's Day*. Below is a list of enjoyable activities that you can do at home with your child. Please support your child's learning by using these activities or by creating some of your own. Your help is greatly appreciated.

Suggested Activities:

- Ask your child what makes someone a mother. Ask what types of things a mother might do. Discuss these with your child.

- Take your child to the public library. Check out a storybook or nonfiction book about Mother's Day. Read it together. Discuss your favorite parts with one another.

- Each of you can draw and color a picture of a mother and a child. Tell about your pictures.

- Tell your child something special you remember about your mother or a mother figure from when you were young.

- Tell your child a story about something your mother did when she was your child's age.

- Read "What Is a Mother?" with your child. Together, pantomime how mothers do the different things described in the poem.

Best wishes,

_____

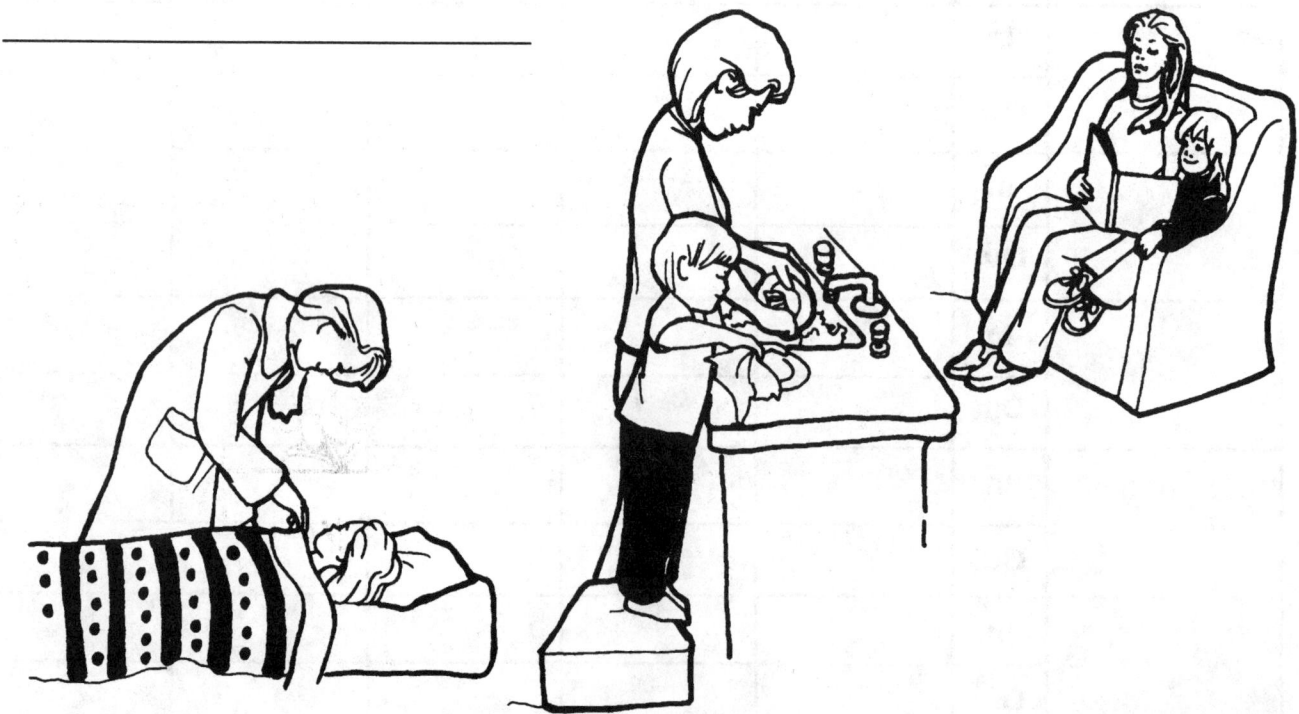

Mother's Day   Thematic Activities

Mother's Day Arts and Crafts I

Have students follow the directions shown below to make a special note or flower holder for Mother's Day.

Materials:

- glue
- scissors
- glitter
- paper or Styrofoam plates (2 per student)
- markers or paints and paintbrushes
- yarn

Directions:

1. Give each student two plates. Help students cut one of their plates in half.
2. On the chalkboard, write the words "I love you." Ask students to copy these words on one of their half plates.
3. Have students glue the half plate with "I love you" on it to the whole plate so the back sides are facing out. This will create a pocket.
4. Encourage students to decorate their holders, using markers, paints, and/or glitter.
5. Poke a hole at the top of each whole plate. Then string a loop of yarn through it so that the holder can be hung up.
6. Have students place a special note, a drawing, or some flowers in the pocket.

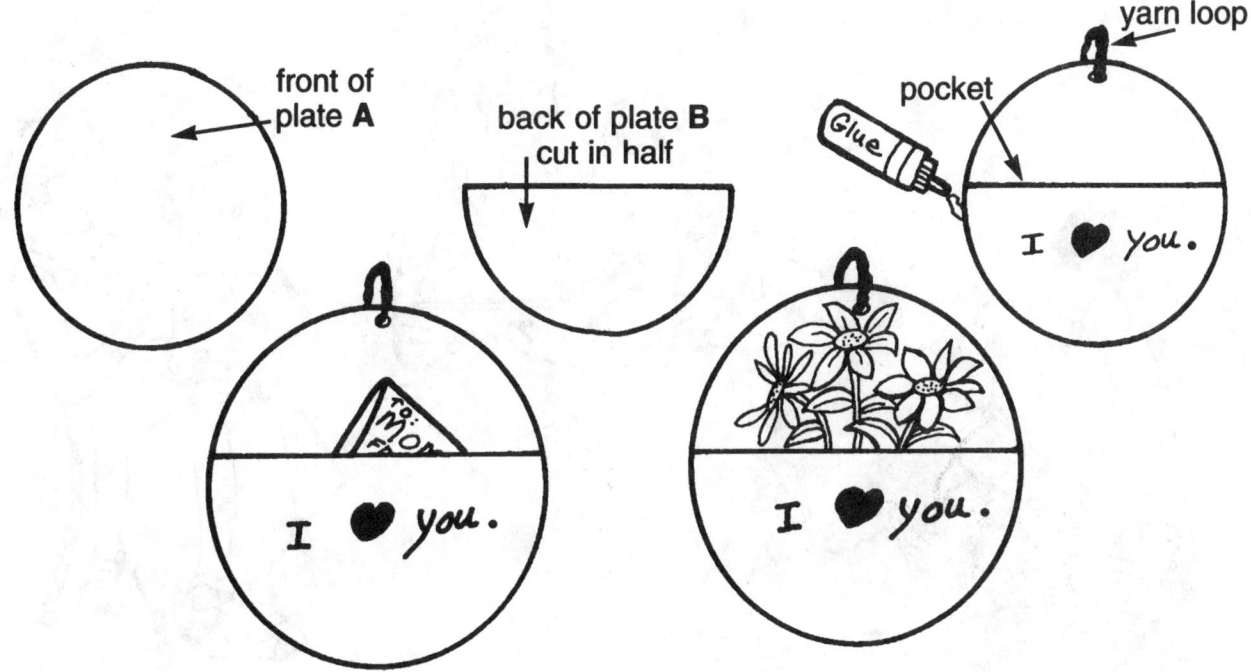

Mother's Day   Thematic Activities

Mother's Day Arts and Crafts II

In this activity, students make a Mother's Day collage for the classroom.

Materials:

- old magazines
- scissors (optional)
- glue
- large poster board

Directions:

1. Ask parents to send a variety of magazines, especially those on parenting. Let parents know that the magazines are for an art project, and they will not be returned. You might wish to ask for a photograph of each student with his or her mother, grandmother, or another significant female caretaker.

2. Let students tear (or cut) out pictures of mothers and children (including animal mothers and their young) from the magazines.

3. Allow students to glue their pictures onto the poster board to create a class collage. You may prefer to have each student make a collage. If so, provide a piece of poster board for each student.

4. Write "Mother Means Love" at the top of the collage.

5. Display the collage in the classroom, hallway, or library.

Mother's Day / *Thematic Activities*

Mother's Day Story

As a class, read *I Love My Mommy Because . . .* by Laurel Porter-Gaylord (Dutton Children's Books, 1991). Then, give each student a copy of the frame shown below. Have them dictate an end to the sentence as you write it. Ask students to draw pictures of the mothers. Staple the pages together with a title page that reads, "We Love Our Mommies Because . . . ."

I love my mommy because _____

_____.

Mother's Day   Thematic Activities

Mother's Day Letters

Practice the letter M for *mother*. Have students color these giant M's. Have them pretend that the uppercase M is the mother of the lowercase m. Ask what sort of things the M's might say to one another. Then ask what these two M's might do together.

A reward badge for this activity can be found on page 41.

Mother's Day   Thematic Activities

Mother's Day Numbers

Two is an important number for Mother's Day because a mother and child make a set of two. Draw lines to connect each set of two things that go together. The first one is done for you.

©1995 Teacher Created Materials, Inc.   31   #868 May Monthly Activities—Early Childhood

Mother's Day — *Thematic Activities*

Mother's Day Colors

Many children equate a mother with love. Since red is considered the color of love, invite students to experiment with it.

Materials:

- red tempera paint, premixed
- paper plates or bowls
- large white paper (1 per student)
- sponges cut into heart shapes (1 per student)
- old shirts or smocks (1 per student)
- red markers

Directions:

1. Inform parents ahead of time of the date for this project since it will be a messy day. You can send parents a note on the Mother's Day stationery (page 38), asking them to send old shirts or smocks if you do not already have some.

2. Give each student a red marker and a piece of paper folded in half to make a card.

3. On the chalkboard or a large sheet of paper, write the words "I love you." Ask students to copy those words inside their cards. Then, help them write their names.

4. Give each student a smock, a sponge, and some red paint on a paper plate or bowl. Have them dab the heart-shaped sponges in the paint and then stamp red hearts on the covers of their cards. Let the paint dry.

5. Send the cards home for Mother's Day.

6. A badge for this activity can be found on page 41.

Mother's Day   Thematic Activities

Mother's Day Shapes

Heart-shaped flowers will be a special treat for moms. Have students color these hearts. After they are finished coloring, help students cut out the hearts and glue them onto colored construction paper for the background. Invite students to each make a bouquet of love by drawing stems and leaves with crayons.

©1995 Teacher Created Materials, Inc.   33   #868 May Monthly Activities—Early Childhood

Mother's Day Music

It will be fun for the class to sing some original songs for Mother's Day. Try one or both of the following.

Mother, Mother, I Love You

(Sing to the tune: "Twinkle, Twinkle, Little Star")

Mother, Mother, I love you,

And I know you love me, too.

Lots of hugs you give to me,

And my mom you'll always be.

Mother, Mother, I love you,

And I know you love me, too.

Mom, Mom, Mom Loves Me

(Sing to the tune: "Row, Row, Row Your Boat")

Mom, Mom, Mom loves me,

Yes, I know it's true.

Happily, happily, happily, happily,

And I love her, too.

Mother's Day   *Thematic Activities*

Mother's Day Food

Make some "love toast" in your classroom and teach students how to make it at home for their mothers on Mother's Day. You can give them the recipe card below to take home.

Note: Ask parents if their children have any dietary restrictions or food allergies before using this activity.

Ingredients and Materials:
- sliced white bread (1 slice per student)
- red food coloring
- clean paintbrushes (1 per student)
- milk
- toaster
- bowl

Directions:
1. Pour some milk into the bowl.
2. Add a few drops of food coloring and stir.
3. Give each student a slice of bread.
4. Give each student a paintbrush. Let each use the milk and food coloring mixture to paint a heart on the bread.
5. Toast the bread on a light setting and enjoy!

Love Toast

Ingredients and Materials:
- 1 slice white bread
- red food coloring
- toaster
- milk
- 1 clean paintbrush
- bowl

Directions:
1. Pour some milk into the bowl.
2. Add a few drops of food coloring and stir.
3. Take the slice of bread.
4. Take the paintbrush. Use the milk and food coloring mixture to paint a heart on the bread.
5. Toast the bread on a light setting and enjoy!

©1995 Teacher Created Materials, Inc.   #868 May Monthly Activities—Early Childhood

Mother's Day   *Just for Fun*

Mother and Child

Connect the mothers to their babies.

Mother's Day　　　　　　　　　　　　　　　　　　　　　　　Poem

What Is a Mother?

A poem about mothers
Certainly says a lot,
Because moms are many things—
There isn't much they're not.

They help us with our homework
And kiss away our hurt,
They cook when we are hungry
And clean up all our dirt.

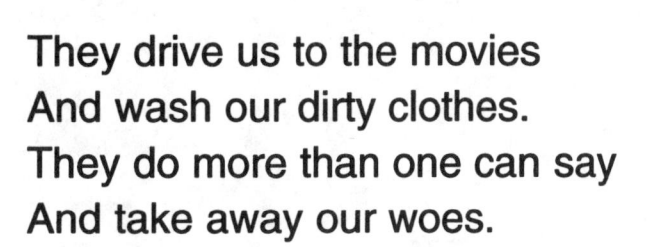

They drive us to the movies
And wash our dirty clothes.
They do more than one can say
And take away our woes.

They paper train our puppies
And shop for all our food.
They cuddle and they hug us
No matter what their mood.

Though many people do these jobs
Mom's not the only one,
I'm so glad the world has moms
To get these jobs all done!

Mother's Day

Stationery

#868 May Monthly Activities—Early Childhood ©1995 Teacher Created Materials, Inc.

Patterns *Mother's Day*

Clip Art and Patterns

Have students fill in the features of the paper doll patterns to make themselves and their mothers, grandmothers, or other significant female caretakers.

©1995 Teacher Created Materials, Inc. #868 May Monthly Activities—Early Childhood

Mother's Day Patterns

Clip Art and Patterns (cont.)

#868 May Monthly Activities—Early Childhood ©1995 Teacher Created Materials, Inc.

Mother's Day   Rewards

Bookmarks and Badges

I know the color red.

Have students color the crayon red and wear their badges home.

I know the letter M.

Let students color their badges and wear them home.

I love my mom

Have students choose their favorite flowers and then color their badges. They can wear the badges home.

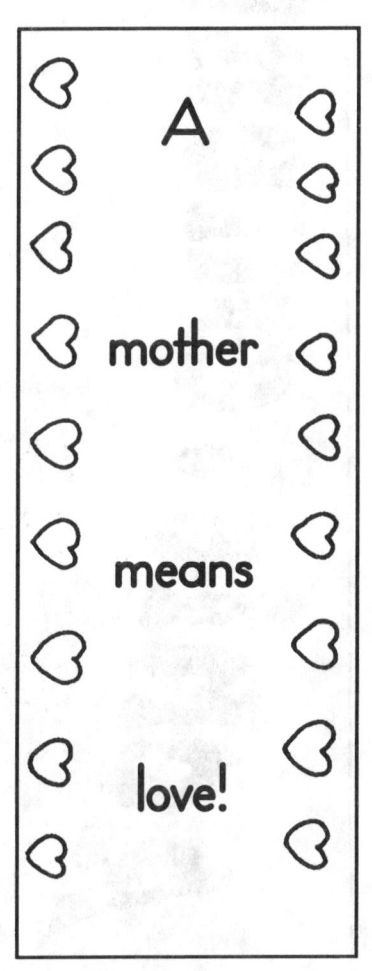

Let's read about mothers.

A mother means love!

Although most early childhood students have not yet learned to read, they enjoy having bookmarks to use while reading with their families at home.

©1995 Teacher Created Materials, Inc.   41   #868 May Monthly Activities—Early Childhood

Mother's Day   *Award*

Achievement Award

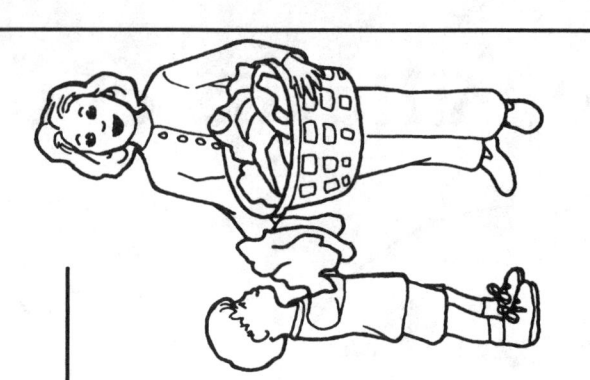

has earned our

Classroom Achievement Award

for

BEING A GOOD HELPER!

_____ _____
Teacher's Signature   Date

#868 May Monthly Activities—Early Childhood   42   ©1995 Teacher Created Materials, Inc.

Caterpillars and Butterflies

Lesson-Planning Sheet

Activity (circle time, playtime, etc.)	Monday	Tuesday	Wednesday	Thursday	Friday

©1995 Teacher Created Materials, Inc. #868 May Monthly Activities—Early Childhood

Caterpillars and Butterflies   **Daily Attendance**

Parent Sign In/Out Sheet

Parents: Please sign your child in and out under the current date.

Name	Time	Date:	Date:	Date:	Date:	Date:
	In					
	Out					
	In					
	Out					
	In					
	Out					
	In					
	Out					
	In					
	Out					
	In					
	Out					
	In					
	Out					
	In					
	Out					
	In					
	Out					
	In					
	Out					

Caterpillars and Butterflies   Home Activities

Caterpillars and Butterflies Activities for Home

Dear Parents and Guardians,

Our theme of the week is *Caterpillars and Butterflies*. Below is a list of enjoyable activities that you can do with your child. Please support your child's learning by using these activities or by creating some of your own. Your help is greatly appreciated.

Suggested Activities:

- Plant a butterfly garden. Your local nursery will know which type of flowers will most likely attract butterflies.

- Go on a butterfly hunt. Remind your child to look but not touch. Touching will harm the butterfly.

- Go on a hunt for caterpillars. Let your child hold the caterpillar carefully in his or her hand and then return the caterpillar to its natural habitat.

- Take your child to the public library. Check out a storybook or nonfiction book about a caterpillar or butterfly. Read it together. Discuss your favorite parts with one another.

- Imagine together that you are caterpillars. Move as caterpillars do, roll yourselves into "cocoons," and then become butterflies.

- Each of you can draw and color a picture of a caterpillar and/or a butterfly. Tell about your pictures.

- Discuss the differences between caterpillars and butterflies.

- Read "The Caterpillar" with your child. Let your child act it out as you read aloud.

Best wishes,

_____

Caterpillars and Butterflies Arts and Crafts I

No lesson on caterpillars would be complete without making the traditional egg carton caterpillar. To fill your classroom with these creepy crawlers, use the following directions.

Materials:

- tempera paint
- paintbrushes
- scissors
- tape (optional)
- cardboard egg carton (1 per 4 students)
- chenille sticks (2 halves and 6 thirds per student)
- old shirts or smocks (1 per student)

Directions:

1. Inform parents ahead of time of the date for this project since it will be a messy day. You can send parents a note on the caterpillar and butterfly stationery (page 57), asking them to send old shirts or smocks if you do not already have some.

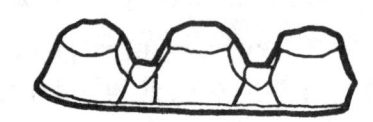

2. Prepare the egg cartons ahead of time by cutting off the tops and saving them for another project or discarding them. Then, cut each bottom portion in half lengthwise and widthwise so that you have four rows with three cups in each.

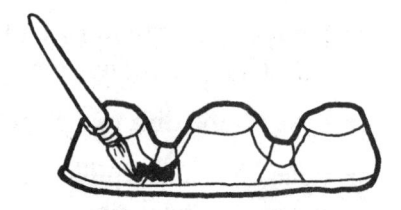

3. Give each student a section from the bottom of the carton. Tell students to turn their sections upside down so that the hollows of the cups cannot be seen. Point out that these are the caterpillars' bodies.

4. Let each student paint his or her caterpillar's body in any way desired.

5. Allow the paint to dry. After a caterpillar is dry, poke a small hole in each side of the three body sections for the legs and two holes at the top of the front section for the antennae.

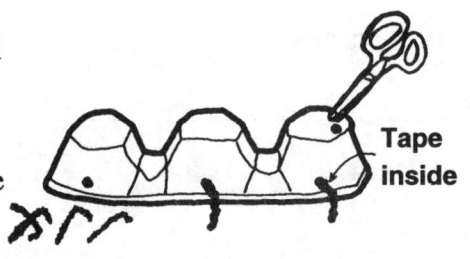

6. Give each student the six pieces of the chenille stick that have been cut into thirds and two pieces that have been cut into halves. The halves should be inserted in the two top holes as the antennae. The thirds should be placed in the side holes as the legs. To hold the chenille sticks in place, insert each piece far enough through a hole in the carton so that the end can be bent downwards inside the cup. If desired, tape over the ends of the chenille sticks in order to better secure them.

7. Let each student paint on additional features. Allow the paint to dry. Then, display the caterpillars.

Caterpillars and Butterflies Arts and Crafts II

Use the following directions to make butterflies that complement the caterpillars (page 46).

Materials:

- white and colored construction paper
- butterfly pattern (page 48)
- colored plastic wrap
- scissors
- glue
- crayons
- chenille sticks (cut into halves)

Directions:

1. Reproduce the butterfly pattern (page 48) on white and colored construction paper. Give each student one white and one colored butterfly pattern that has been pre-cut or let students cut out their own. These butterfly patterns should have the center sections cut out.
2. Let students use glue to trace over the back of the colored butterfly.
3. Have students carefully lay a piece of colored plastic wrap on top of the glue, covering the entire butterfly.
4. Let students use glue to retrace the back of the colored butterfly, this time over the plastic.
5. Have them lay the white butterfly over the glue on the plastic, matching the edges to those of the colored butterfly. Allow the glue to dry.
6. Help students trim the excess plastic wrap around the butterfly patterns. Tell them to turn the butterfly so the colored side can be seen. If students desire, they can use crayons to add a face and chenille stick halves to add antennae.
7. Hang and display the butterflies in a window.

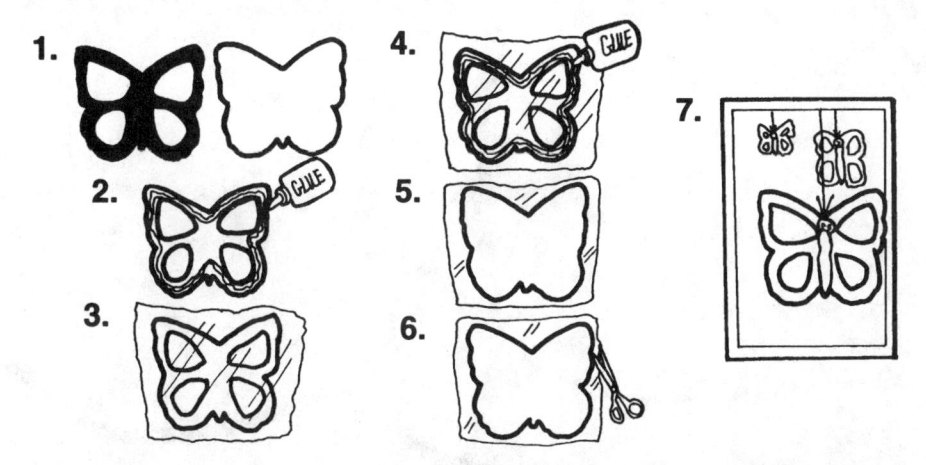

Extension: Place each student's butterfly in a brown paper sack. Hang the sacks around the room and call them cocoons. Let each student place his or her caterpillar (page 46) in the cocoon and then pull out the butterfly.

Caterpillars and Butterflies Arts and Crafts II *(cont.)*

Caterpillars and Butterflies   Thematic Activities

Caterpillars and Butterflies Story

As a class, read *The Very Hungry Caterpillar* by Eric Carle (Putnam, 1969). Then, create a classroom book that goes along with the story.

Materials:

- standard-size white paper
- crayons
- glue
- scissors
- caterpillar pattern (shown below, 1 per student)
- butterfly pattern (page 58, optional)
- stapler or brads

Directions:

1. Give each student one sheet of white paper. At the top of each paper, write "The caterpillar ate . . . ." and conclude it by asking each student to name a food from the story or his or her favorite food.

2. Let each student draw and color a picture of the food that he or she named to complete the sentence.

3. Reproduce the caterpillar pattern shown at the bottom of the page. Give each student a copy of the pattern. Tell students to color their patterns, cut them out, and then glue the caterpillars to their food pictures.

4. On an additional piece of white paper, draw an outline of a butterfly. You can use the pattern on page 58 if desired. Invite each student to help color the butterfly picture so that it is a group effort.

5. Make a cover for the book. Staple or brad all the pages together, placing the butterfly picture last. Share the book with the class, allowing each student to read his or her page.

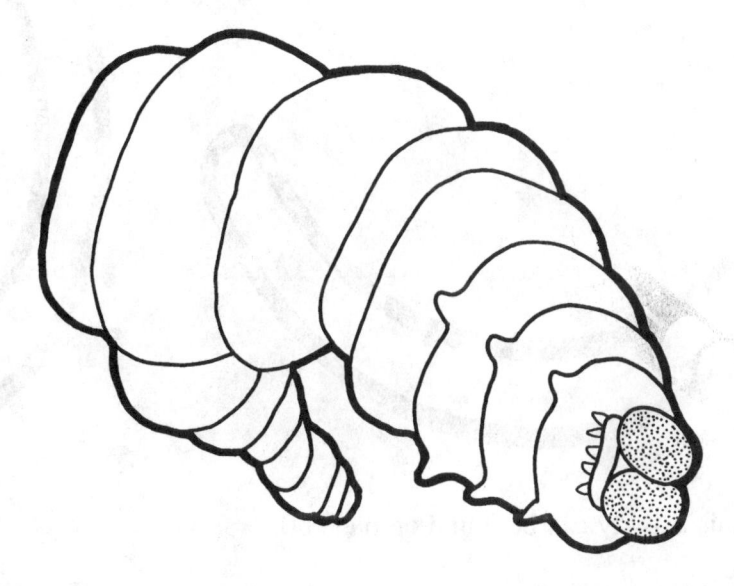

©1995 Teacher Created Materials, Inc.

Caterpillars and Butterflies   *Thematic Activities*

Caterpillars and Butterflies Letters

Practice the letter **C** for caterpillars. Have students color these giant C's. Ask them if they can make the C's look like caterpillars. To do so, they can add lines and details of their own. Then, they can color two pictures of butterflies on the back of the paper to show the butterflies that the caterpillars will become.

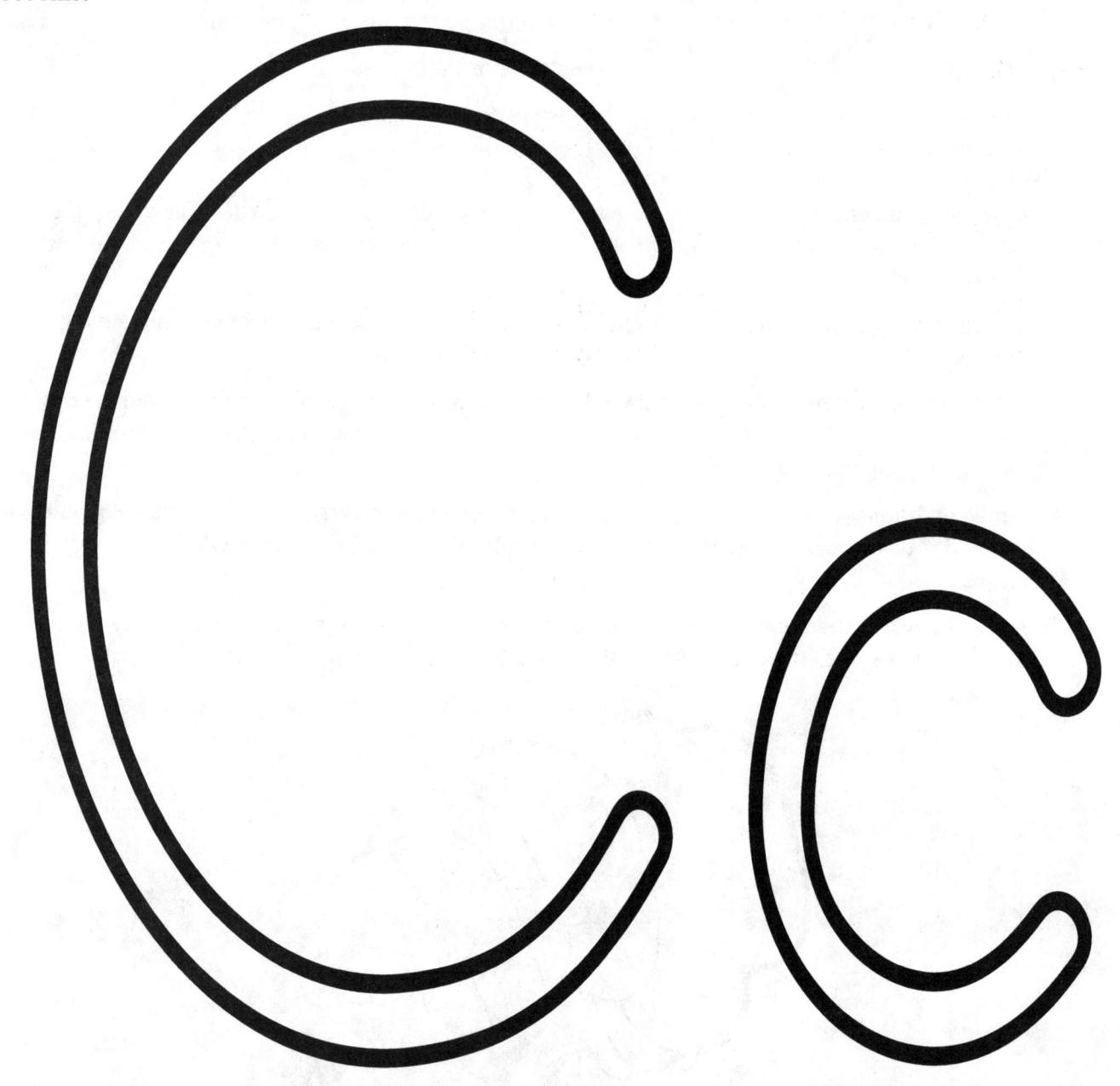

A reward badge for this activity can be found on page 60.

Caterpillars and Butterflies   Thematic Activities

Caterpillars and Butterflies Colors

Yellow is a color very commonly found on butterflies. Invite students to experiment with yellow as they make some butterflies of their own.

Materials:

- yellow construction paper
- butterfly pattern (page 58, 1 per student)
- glue
- crayons

Directions:

1. Reproduce the butterfly pattern (page 58). Give each student a butterfly pattern and a sheet of yellow construction paper. Point out that the paper is colored yellow. Ask students to name other things that are yellow.

2. Have students tear the yellow paper into small pieces. Explain that they will use these pieces to make a butterfly mosaic.

3. Have students glue the pieces over the pattern, completely filling in the butterfly shape.

4. When the glue is dry, let students use crayons to add the butterfly's features.

5. Hang the butterflies around the classroom.

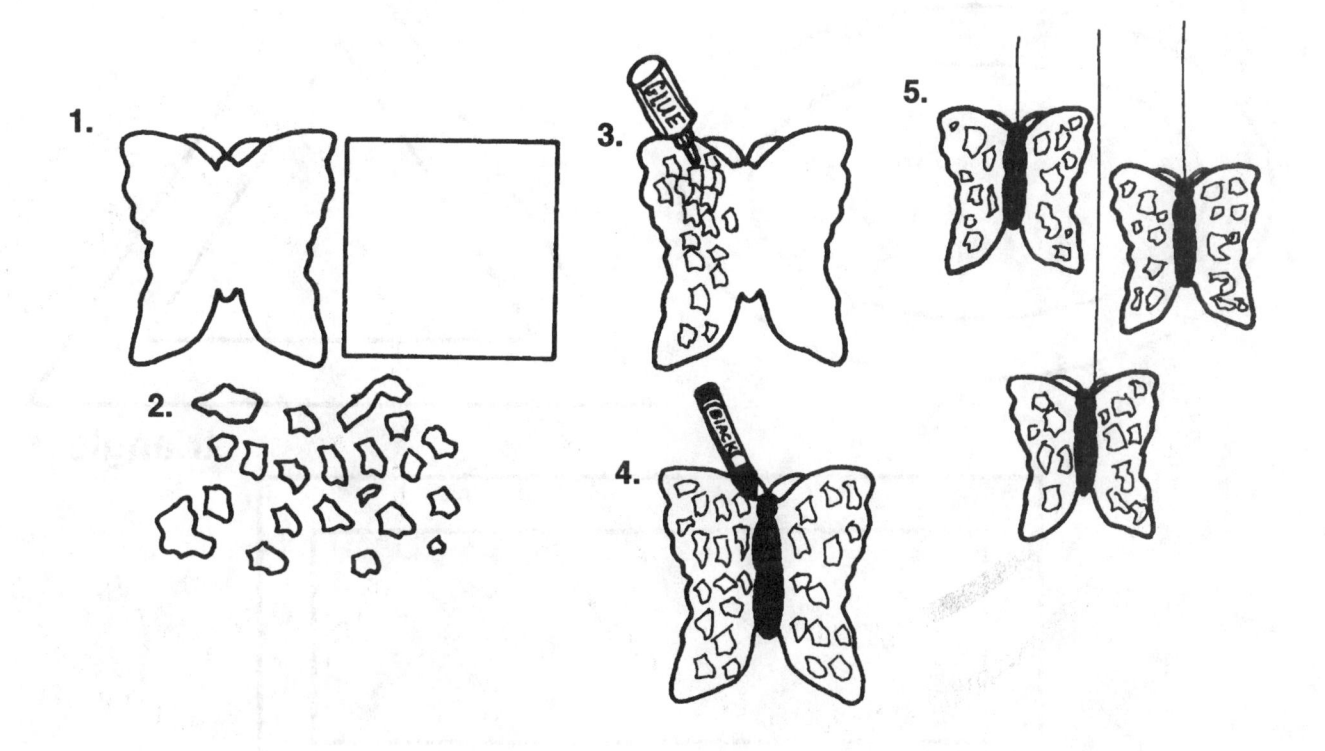

©1995 Teacher Created Materials, Inc.   51   #868 May Monthly Activities—Early Childhood

Caterpillars and Butterflies *Thematic Activities*

Caterpillars and Butterflies Shapes

Invite students to use "caterpillars" to form different shapes. You will need to reproduce this page and provide chenille sticks. Give each student a copy of this page and five chenille sticks. Tell students to pretend that the chenille sticks are "caterpillars." One by one, let students bend the sticks over the shapes, naming each shape as they do so.

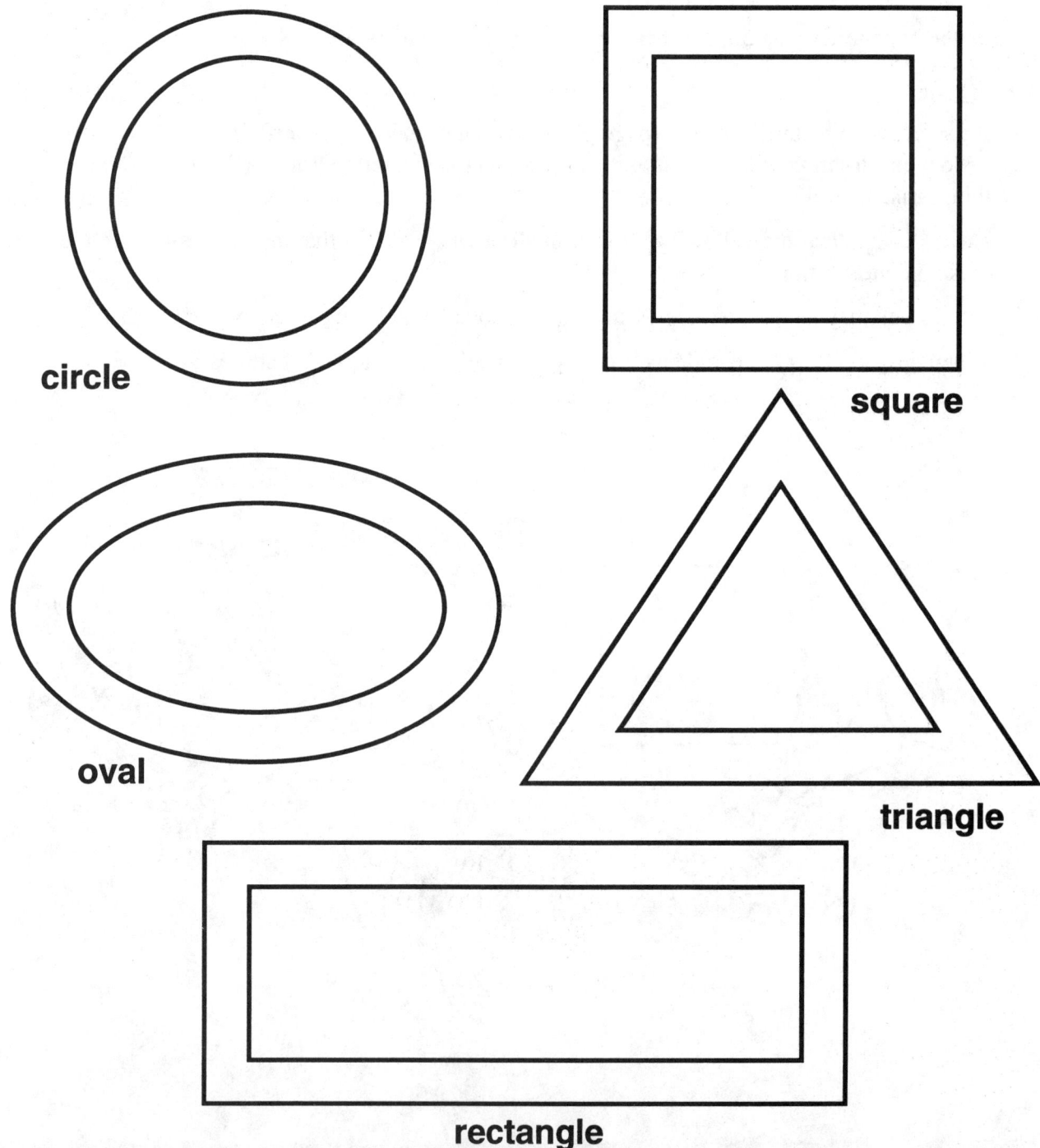

circle

square

oval

triangle

rectangle

Caterpillars and Butterflies Movements

Have students form a giant caterpillar and, together, turn into butterflies. Follow these steps:

1. Ask students to stand in a line. Have students place their hands on the shoulders of the students standing in front of them. Remind students to follow safety rules as they move around the classroom for this activity.

2. Students can make the giant caterpillar walk by moving their feet in unison, first their right and then their left feet, and continuing in that manner. Remind them to pay careful attention in order to move together.

3. After they move around the classroom once or twice as described in Step 2, direct students to form a "cocoon." To do so, students should move together to a certain section of the classroom and then wrap around closely together. Then you can throw a large sheet, preferably brown or green, over the "cocoon" of students. Tell students that the caterpillar now has a cocoon.

4. Say the word *butterfly* and have students throw off the sheet and come out flapping their wings. Tell students that they are now butterflies. They can practice flitting about the classroom and landing on make-believe flowers.

Caterpillars and Butterflies   *Thematic Activities*

Caterpillars and Butterflies Food

While students learn about caterpillars becoming butterflies, they can also learn about the concepts *before* and *after*. There are a great many foods that also demonstrate these concepts. Prepare one or several of them, calling the original foods *caterpillars* and the transformed foods *butterflies*. Here are a few you might try:

unpopped popcorn → **popcorn**

dough → **cookies**

uncooked rice → **cooked rice**

dough → **bread**

batter → **cake**

apples → **applesauce**

ice → **water**

Caterpillars and Butterflies   Just for Fun

Caterpillars and Butterflies

Circle the caterpillars and butterflies hidden in the picture. Then, color the picture.

The Caterpillar

A caterpillar on a branch
Had itself a bite
Of a tasty leaf or two
To ease its appetite.

Then it lay upon the branch
And wove with natural skill,
A neat cocoon to snuggle in,
It lay there very still.

And then there was a lovely thing
After time passed by.
From down inside the old cocoon
Emerged a butterfly!

Caterpillars and Butterflies *Stationery*

©1995 Teacher Created Materials, Inc. 57 #868 May Monthly Activities—Early Childhood

Caterpillars and Butterflies *Patterns*

Clip Art and Patterns

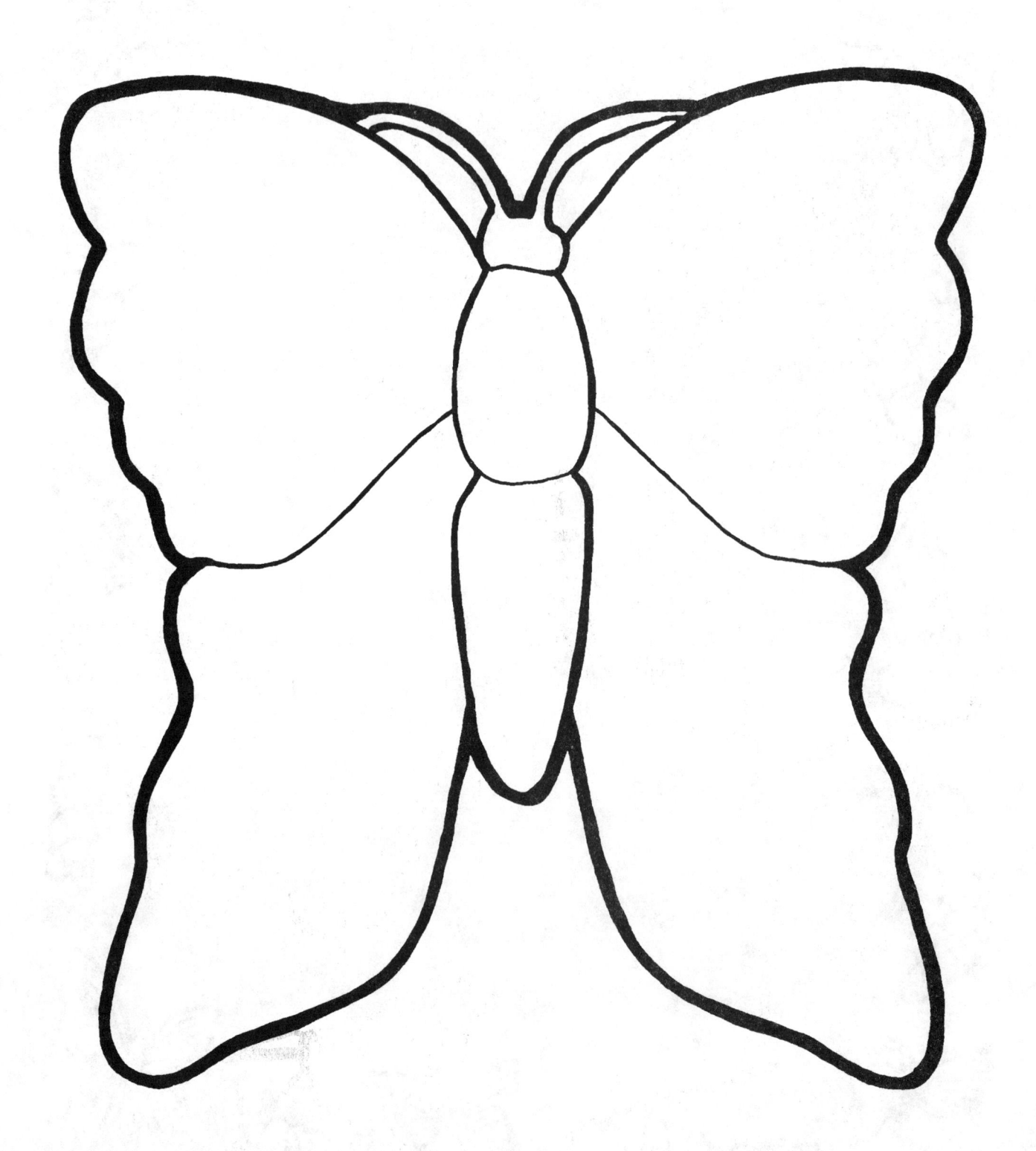

Caterpillars and Butterflies *Patterns*

Clip Art and Patterns *(cont.)*

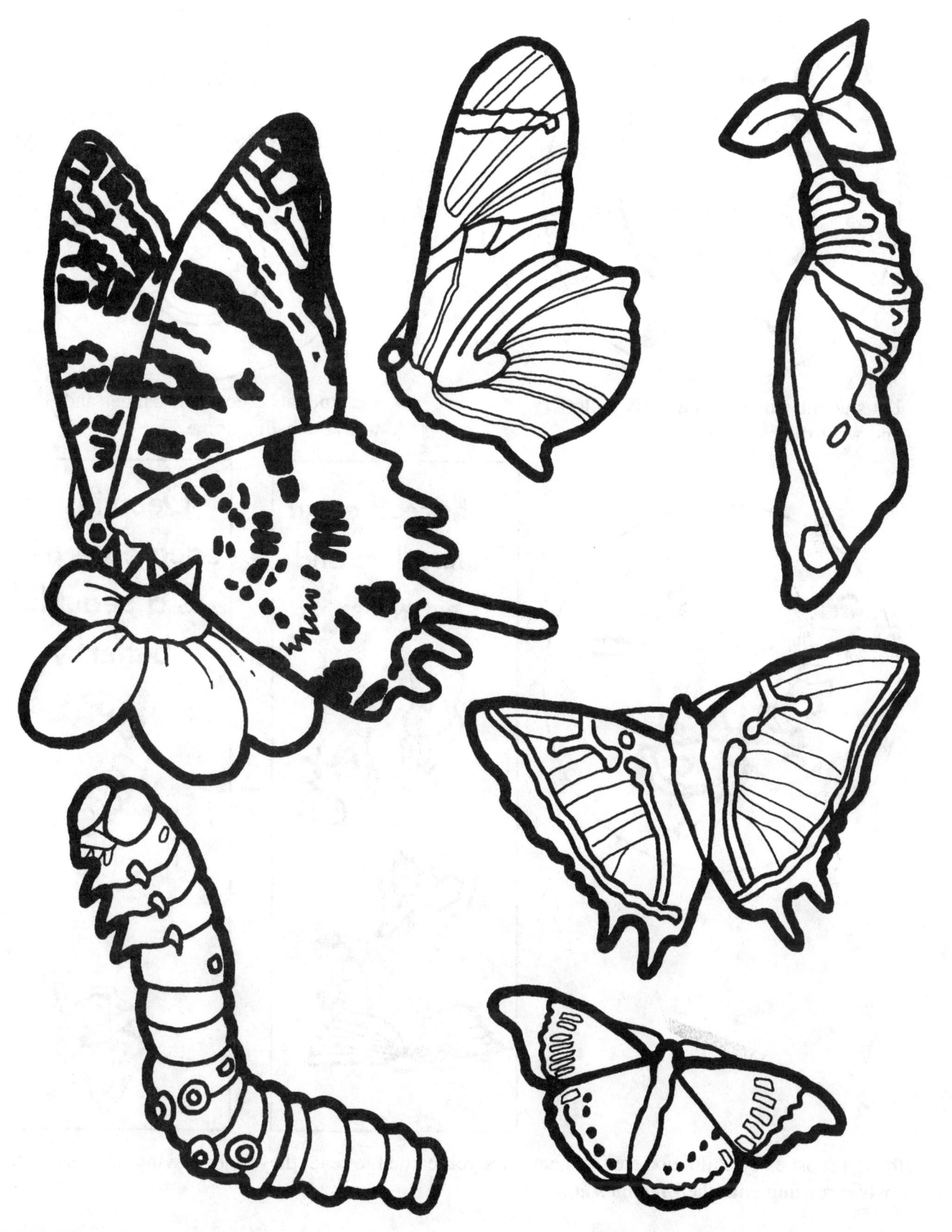

©1995 Teacher Created Materials, Inc. 59 #868 May Monthly Activities—Early Childhood

Caterpillars and Butterflies   *Rewards*

Bookmarks and Badges

I know the color yellow.

I know the letter C.

Let students color the butterfly yellow and wear the badge home.

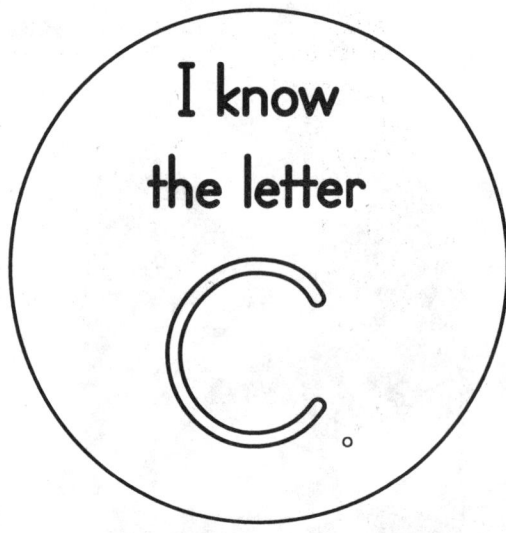

Let students color their badges and wear the badge home.

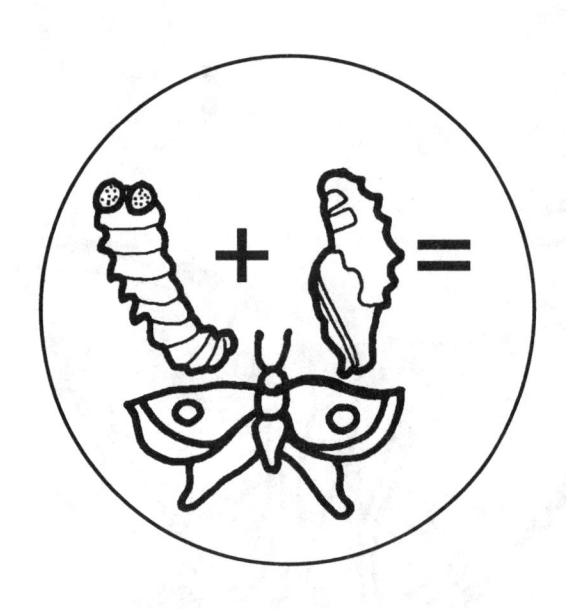

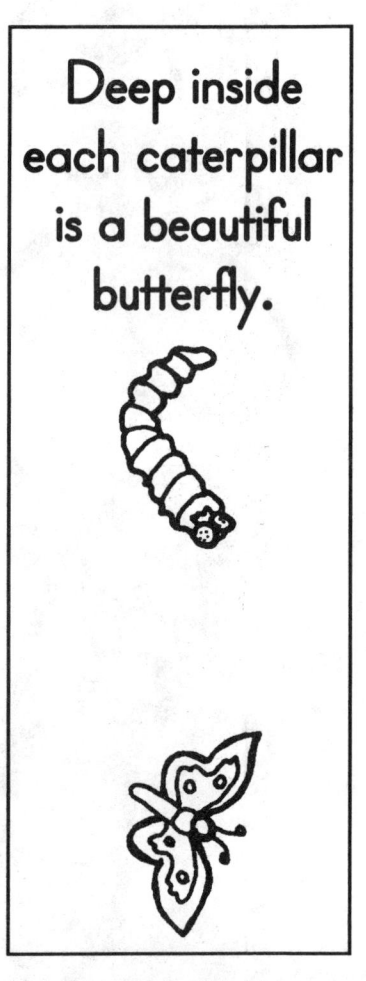

Let's read about caterpillars and butterflies.

Deep inside each caterpillar is a beautiful butterfly.

Although most early childhood students have not yet learned to read, they enjoy having bookmarks to use while reading with their families at home.

Caterpillars and Butterflies — *Award*

Achievement Award

has earned our

Classroom Achievement Award

for

NEATNESS!

_____ Date

_____ Teacher's Signature

©1995 Teacher Created Materials, Inc. — #868 May Monthly Activities—Early Childhood

Trains   Lesson-Planning Sheet

Activity (circle time, playtime, etc.)	Monday	Tuesday	Wednesday	Thursday	Friday

#868 May Monthly Activities—Early Childhood ©1995 Teacher Created Materials, Inc.

Trains **Daily Attendance**

Parent Sign In/Out Sheet

Parents: Please sign your child in and out under the current date.

Name	Time	Date:	Date:	Date:	Date:	Date:
	In					
	Out					
	In					
	Out					
	In					
	Out					
	In					
	Out					
	In					
	Out					
	In					
	Out					
	In					
	Out					
	In					
	Out					
	In					
	Out					

©1995 Teacher Created Materials, Inc. #868 May Monthly Activities—Early Childhood

Trains   *Home Activities*

Train Activities for Home

Dear Parents and Guardians,

This week we will be learning about *trains*. Below is a list of enjoyable activities that you can do at home with your child. Please support your child's learning by using these activities or by creating some of your own. Your help is greatly appreciated.

Suggested Activities:

- Together, pretend that you are trains that live and breathe like the one in *The Little Engine That Could* (Platt and Munk, 1976) by Watty Piper. Imagine the things trains might do as they go through a day and then pantomime those things.
- Take your child to the public library. Check out a storybook or nonfiction book about trains. Read it together. Discuss your favorite parts with one another. (Note: It may be especially interesting to look at pictures that show how trains have changed over time.)
- Each of you can draw and color a picture of a train or a scene with a train. Tell about them.
- Practice making train noises.
- If you have ever ridden on a train, tell your child about the experience. If your child has taken a train ride, discuss it and go over any photographs or scrapbook items you may have.
- If at all possible, take a ride on a train.
- Drive around your town looking for train tracks. Park at a safe distance and watch some trains as they go by.
- Visit a train yard or depot. Watch the trains come and go. Talk to a conductor.
- Go to a hobby shop. Look at different kinds of model trains.
- Read "Here Comes the Train!" with your child. Let your child pantomime the poem as you read.

Best wishes,

_____

Trains   *Thematic Activities*

Train Arts and Crafts I

A giant train will bring hours of fun to any classroom. Here is how to make your own train as a class project.

Materials:

- large cardboard appliance boxes (computer size; 1 per student, plus 1 more)
- tempera paints
- paintbrushes
- glue
- heavy yarn or rope
- child-size chairs (1 per student)
- train controls (page 66, 1 set per student)
- old shirts or smocks (1 per student)

Directions:

1. Inform parents ahead of time of the date for this project since it will be a messy day. You can send parents a note on the train stationery (page 76), asking them to send old shirts or smocks if you do not already have some.

2. Give each student a box. Explain to students that the boxes will be their cars on the classroom train. Let them paint their boxes in any way they choose. Paint the additional box yourself to use as the engine of the train.

3. Allow the painted boxes to dry. While they are drying, have students color their sets of train controls. After the boxes have dried, have students cut apart and glue their train controls inside their cars.

4. Cut a small hole in the front and back of each box. For the engine, you need only cut a hole in the back. For the last car, you need only cut a hole in the front. Tie and knot a length of rope or yarn from the front hole in one car to the back hole in the next car. Continue in this manner until all cars of the train are hooked together.

5. Place a chair inside each car so everyone will have somewhere to sit.

6. Then, use your giant classroom train to make some imaginary trips to the places of your choice!

Trains *Thematic Activities*

Train Arts and Crafts I *(cont.)*

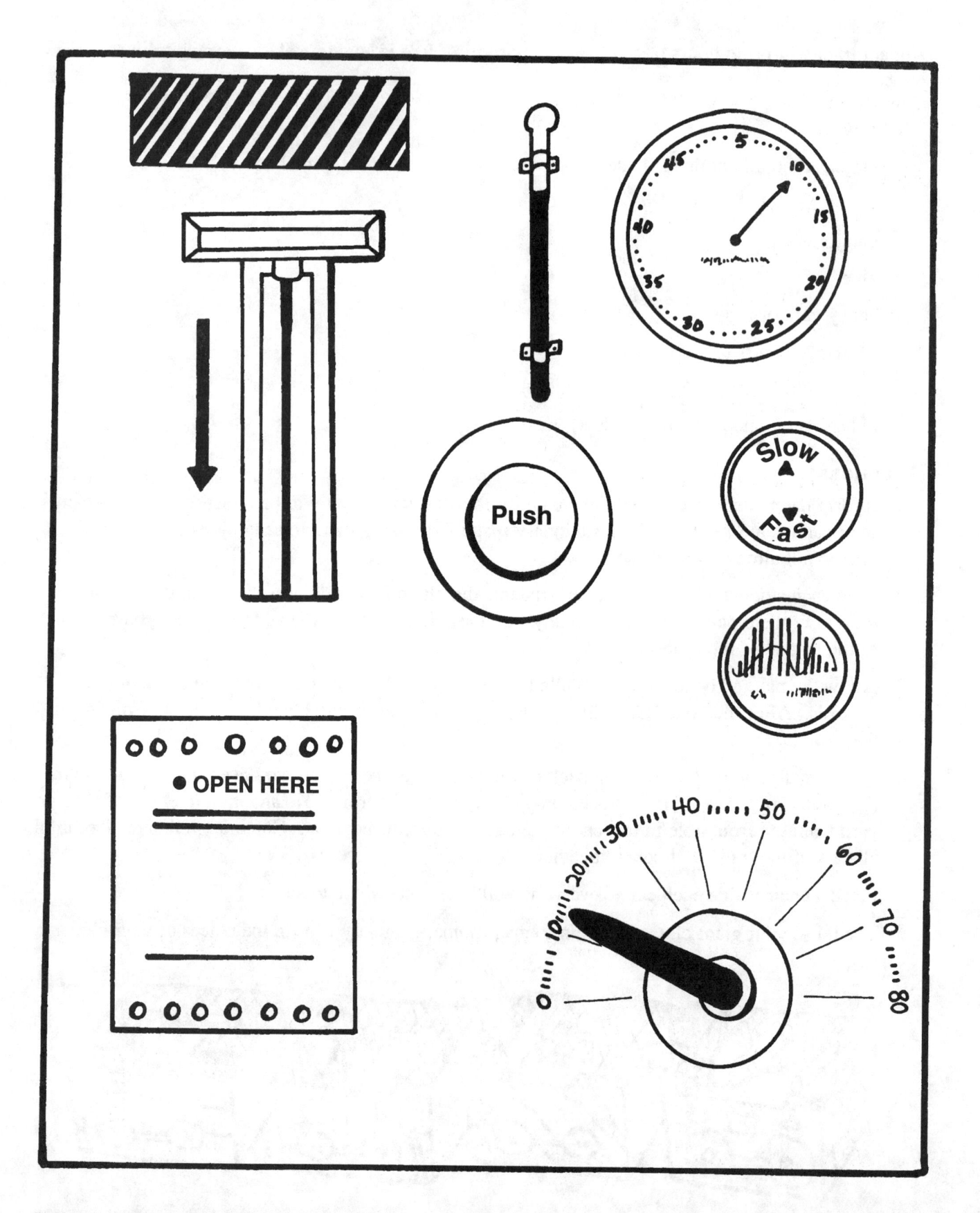

Push

Slow
Fast

OPEN HERE

#868 May Monthly Activities—Early Childhood 66 ©1995 Teacher Created Materials, Inc.

Trains   *Thematic Activities*

Train Story

Students can make a train book to be displayed along one wall of the classroom, using the following directions.

Materials:

- locomotive pattern (page 71*)
- train car pattern (1 per student, page 77*)
- crayons
- tape

*If desired, these patterns can be enlarged.

Directions:

1. Have students sit in a circle. Explain that they will be telling a story about a train, one idea at a time. Each student, in turn, will add a sentence to the story.

2. Begin the story with the sentence, "Once upon a time, there was a train ...."

3. Write the above sentence and all students' sentences on the chalkboard or on a sheet of butcher paper. If possible, have a classroom helper write each student's sentence on a narrow slip of paper, noting on the back the name of the student who suggested it. If no helper is available, you will have to do this in order to complete Step 5.

4. When the story is complete, read it back to students.

5. Glue the slip of paper belonging to each student onto the bottom of a train car pattern. Ask students to illustrate their ideas.

6. When the pictures are complete, use tape to place the train cars together in order along the wall. Make an additional train car and list all students' names on it. Place this train car on the wall in front of the others.

7. Ask students to select a title for the story. Write the title on the locomotive pattern and place it on the wall in front of the train cars.

8. After the book is displayed along the wall of the classroom, invite students to read their pages.

Trains   Thematic Activities

Train Letters

Practice the letter **T** for *train* and *tracks*. Have students color these giant T's. Ask them if they can make the T's look like train tracks. To do so, they can add lines and details of their own.

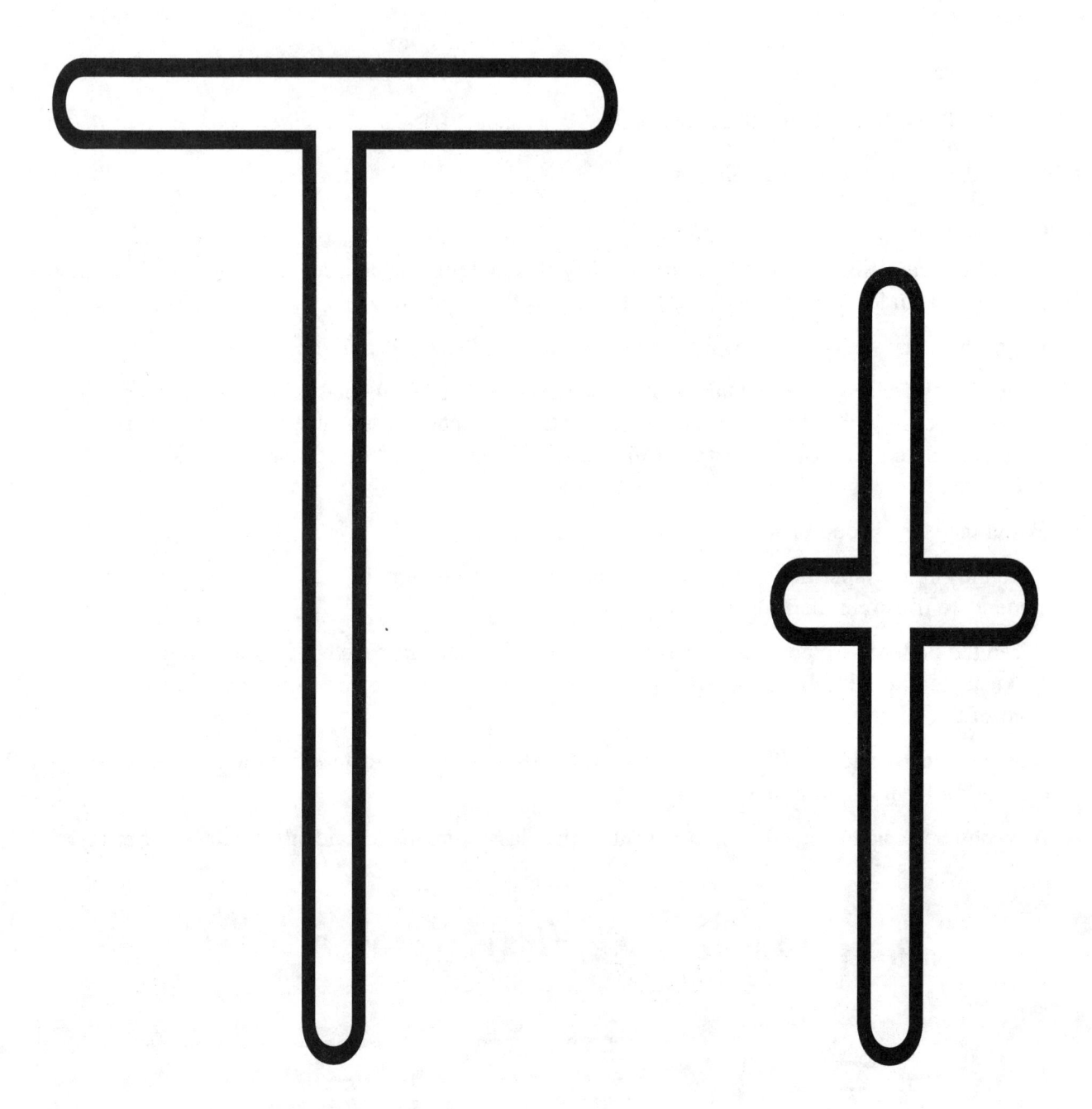

A reward badge for this activity can be found on page 79.

#868 May Monthly Activities—Early Childhood   68   ©1995 Teacher Created Materials, Inc.

Trains   *Thematic Activities*

Train Numbers

This is a physical activity that students will really enjoy. On the playground or on the classroom floor (if it is large enough), make a set of train tracks, using masking tape. Then reproduce the number cards shown below. Cut them apart and place them in a hat, basket, or any other type of container from which students can draw cards. Have students sit on the floor around the tracks. Have students take turns drawing a number, and then move in the train tracks the number of spaces shown on the card. Repeat this activity until each student has had at least two turns.

1	2	3	4
5	6	7	8
9	10	11	12

Trains   *Thematic Activities*

Train Colors

Train engines of old were often painted a shiny, steely black. Let students learn about black by painting some train engines of their own.

Materials:

- black tempera paint
- paintbrushes
- newspapers
- glue
- paper plates or bowls
- small food, gift, and shoe boxes
- old shirts or smocks (1 per student)

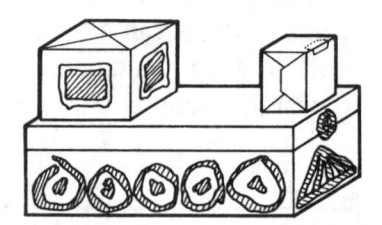

Directions:

1. Inform parents ahead of time of the date for this project since it will be a messy day. You can send parents a note on the train stationery (page 76), asking them to send old shirts or smocks if you do not already have some.

2. Ahead of time, using the boxes, prepare a simple train engine for each student. You can cut and/or stack boxes as needed. The wheels are optional. Glue the boxes together as shown.

   You might also consider letting students construct their own train engines.

3. Spread out some newspapers in front of each student. Give each student a train engine, a smock, a paintbrush, and some black paint in a paper plate or bowl. Point out that the color of the paint is black. Ask students to name different things around them that are black.

4. Ask students to cover their train engines with the black paint.

   Extension: After the black paint is dry, students can paint on other details using additional colors.

   Simplification: Give students the train engine pattern shown on page 77. Enlarge it if desired. Let students use the black paint on their patterns.

Trains *Thematic Activities*

Train Shapes

Have students color and cut out the circle and rectangle shapes on this page. Guide them in gluing the shapes together to form a train, as shown.

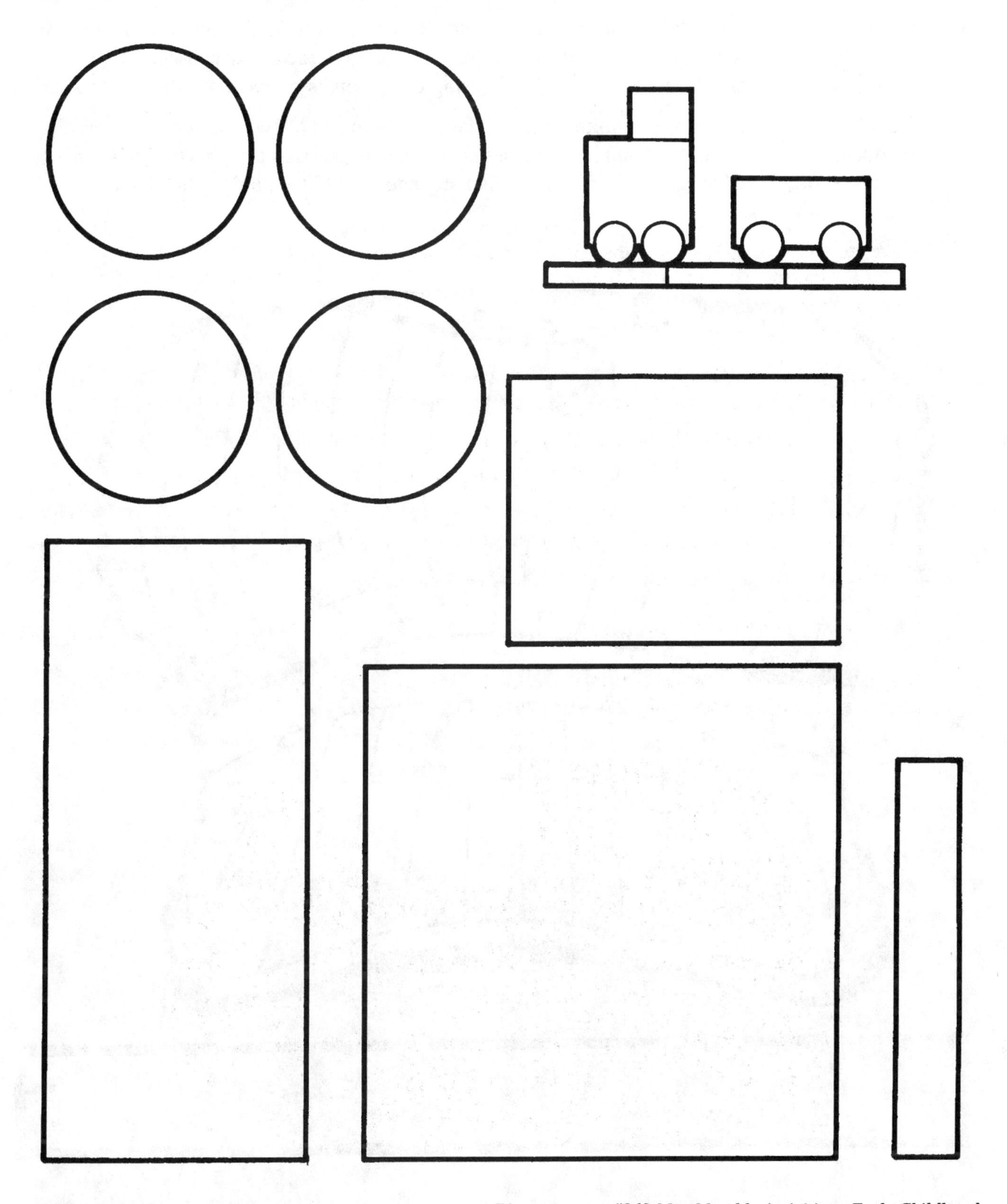

Trains   *Thematic Activities*

Train Music

The sounds with which trains are most associated are whistles. If you have a supply of whistles or easy access to them, try this:

1. Reproduce the conductor's hat shown below. Color the hat, cut it out, and glue it to a headband or attach it to the front of a child-sized baseball cap. Then, give each student a whistle. If whistles are not available, students can whistle using their mouths or make whistling-type sounds.

2. Call each student, one at a time, to the front of the classroom and allow him or her to wear the conductor's hat. Let that student play out a series of whistles, such as two short sounds, one long and one short, three longs, or so forth. The other students should then repeat the conductor's pattern of whistles.

3. Have students take turns being the conductor until everyone has had an opportunity.

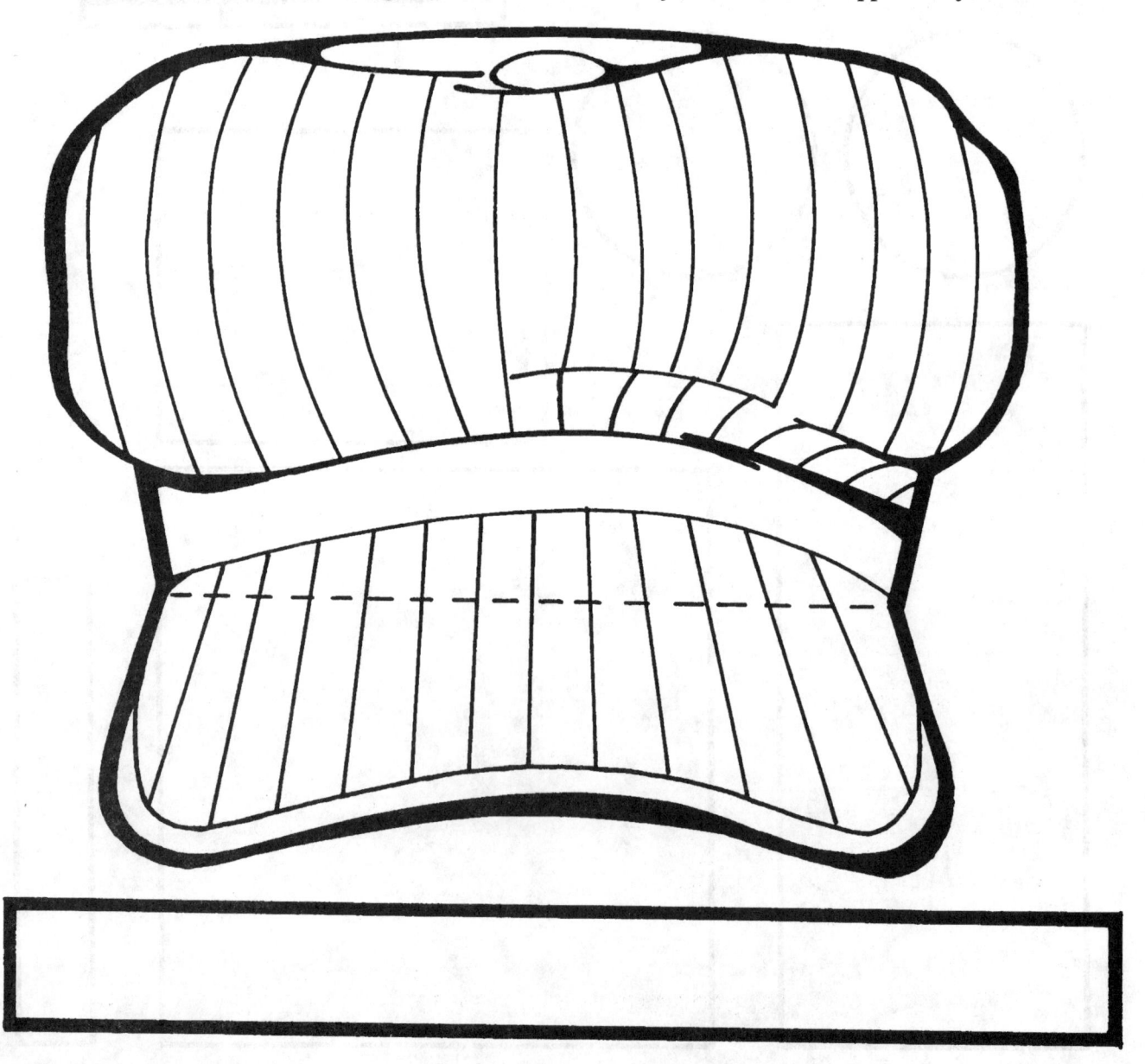

#868 May Monthly Activities—Early Childhood   72   ©1995 Teacher Created Materials, Inc.

Trains *Thematic Activities*

Train Movement

Here is another Follow the Leader activity. Enlarge and reproduce the four cards at the bottom of this page. Make one engine, one caboose, and as many box and passenger cars as there are students in your class, minus three. Color and cut out the cards. Students can do the coloring if you wish. Laminate the cards if possible. Punch two holes in the upper corners of each card and string yarn through them so that each can be worn around the neck.

You will also need a copy of the conductor's hat (page 72), a flashlight disguised as a lantern, and a whistle for the engine. Let one student be the conductor, wearing the hat and carrying the lantern. Let another student be the engine, wearing the engine card and carrying the whistle. Let a third student be the caboose, wearing the caboose card. Ask the rest of the students to be box and passenger cars, wearing the appropriate cards. Students should stand in line in the order of a train: engine, box and passenger cars, and caboose. The conductor will walk down the side of the train, waving the lantern. If desired, the conductor can also punch imaginary or real tickets when walking by the passenger cars. The conductor will call, "All aboard!" and the locomotive will whistle. Next, everyone should move in unison with the locomotive: left foot, right foot, etc. They can say, "Chug, chug," or "Choo, choo," with every step. Challenge them to see how long they can keep this up. If you wish, you can have students rotate positions and repeat this activity.

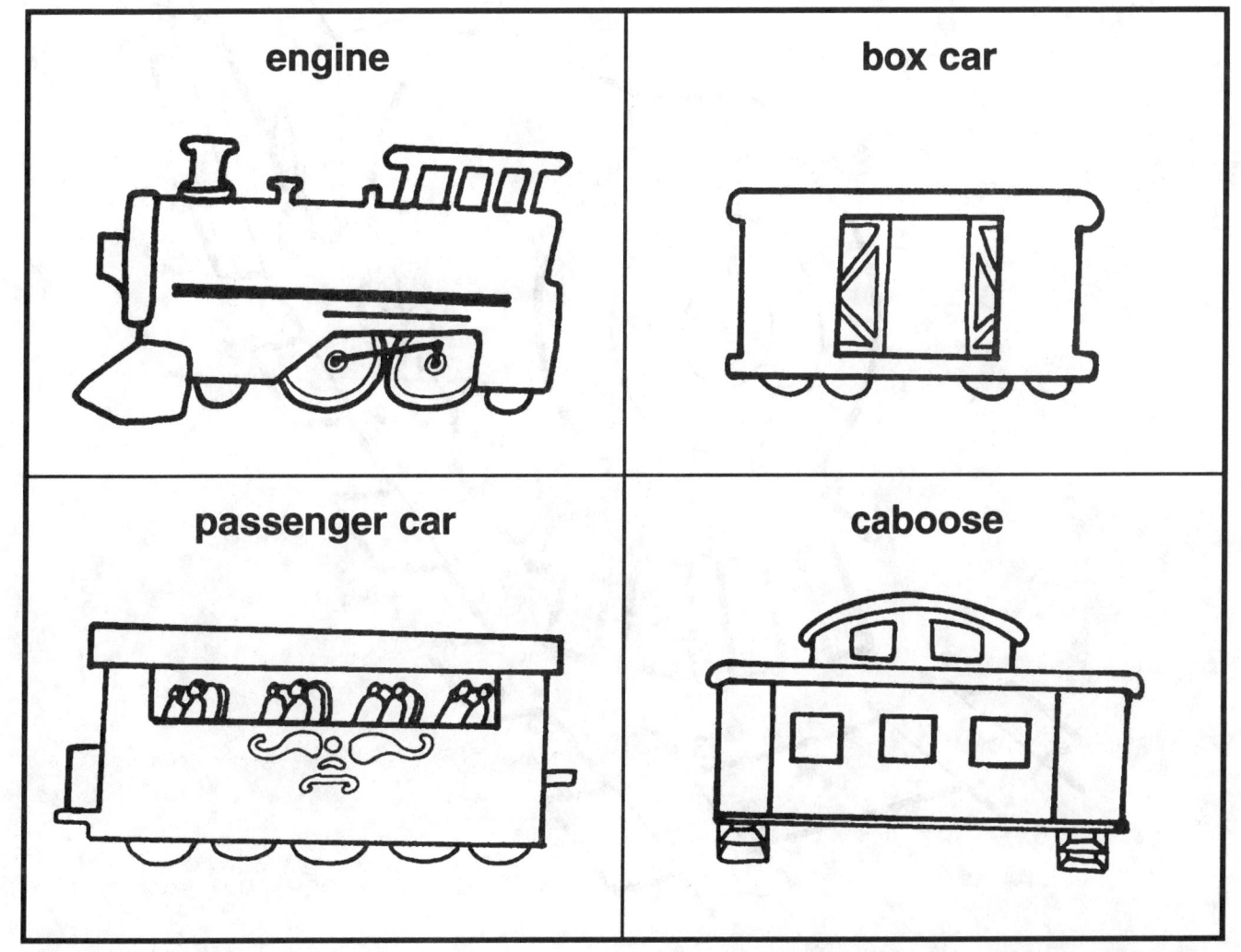

engine

box car

passenger car

caboose

©1995 Teacher Created Materials, Inc.

Trains *Just for Fun*

Down the Tracks

Connect the dots to find the picture. Color.

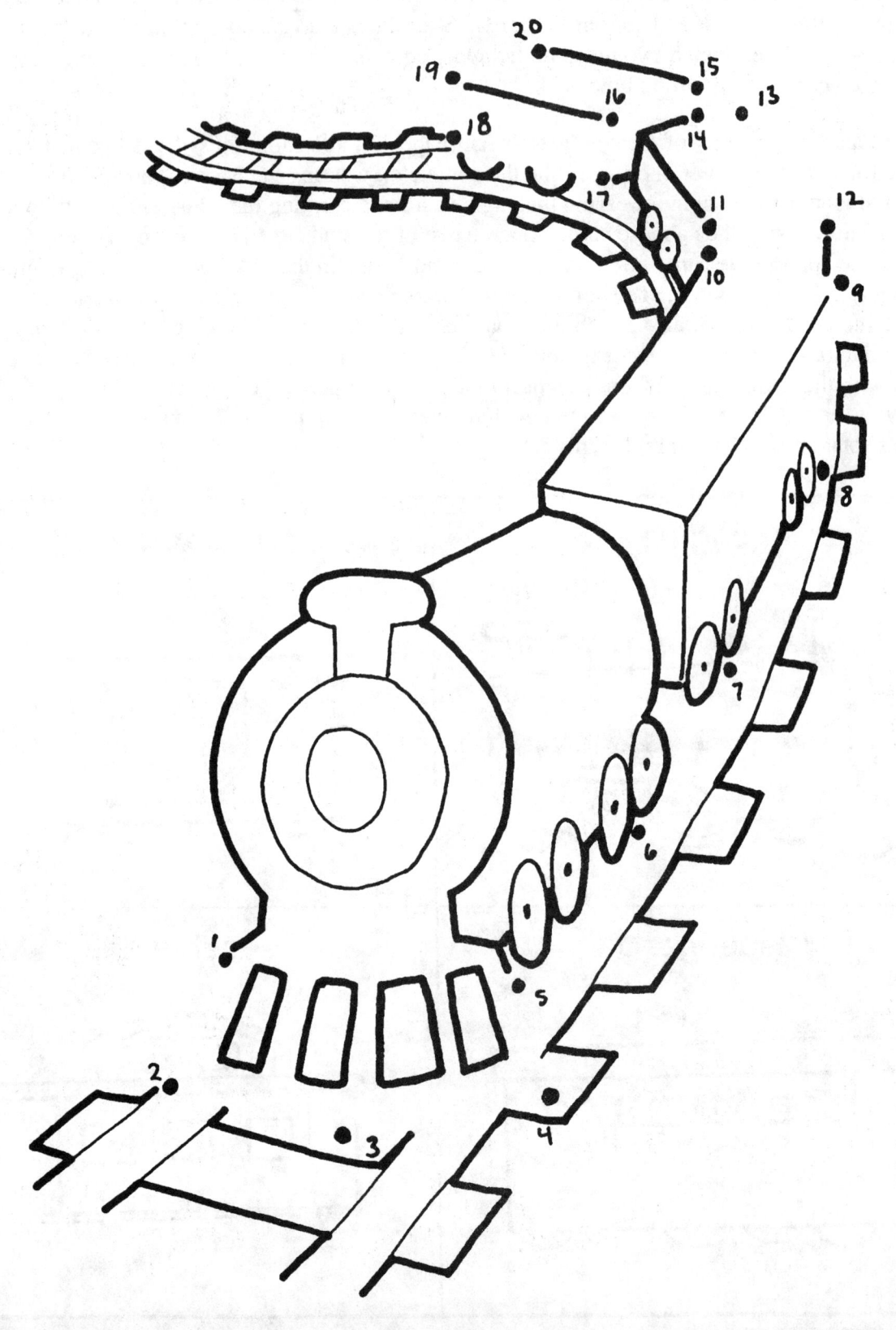

#868 May Monthly Activities—Early Childhood ©1995 Teacher Created Materials, Inc.

Trains   Poem

Here Comes the Train!

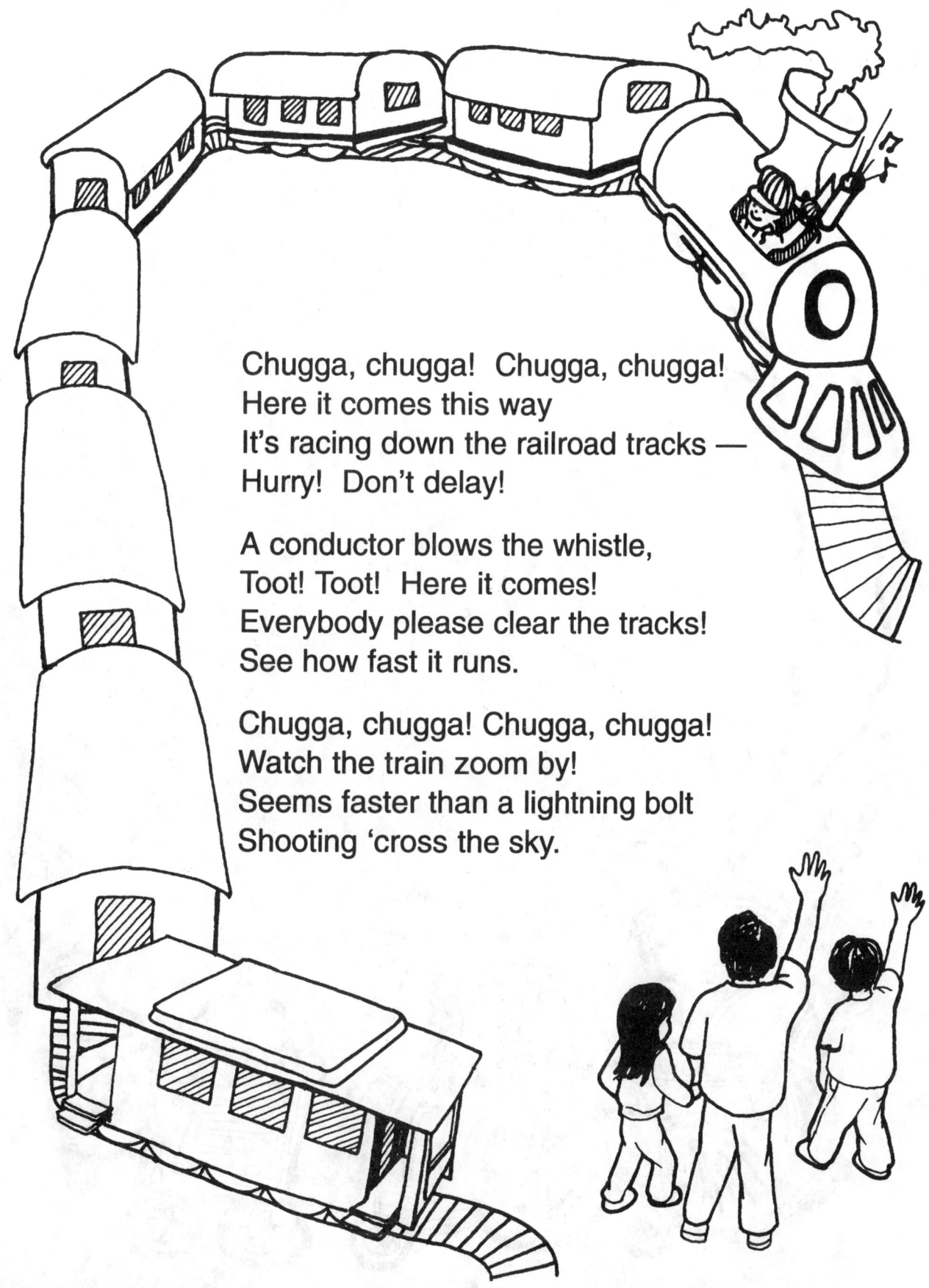

Chugga, chugga! Chugga, chugga!
Here it comes this way
It's racing down the railroad tracks —
Hurry! Don't delay!

A conductor blows the whistle,
Toot! Toot! Here it comes!
Everybody please clear the tracks!
See how fast it runs.

Chugga, chugga! Chugga, chugga!
Watch the train zoom by!
Seems faster than a lightning bolt
Shooting 'cross the sky.

©1995 Teacher Created Materials, Inc.   #868 May Monthly Activities—Early Childhood

Trains *Stationery*

#868 May Monthly Activities—Early Childhood 76 ©1995 Teacher Created Materials, Inc.

Trains *Patterns*

Clip Art and Patterns

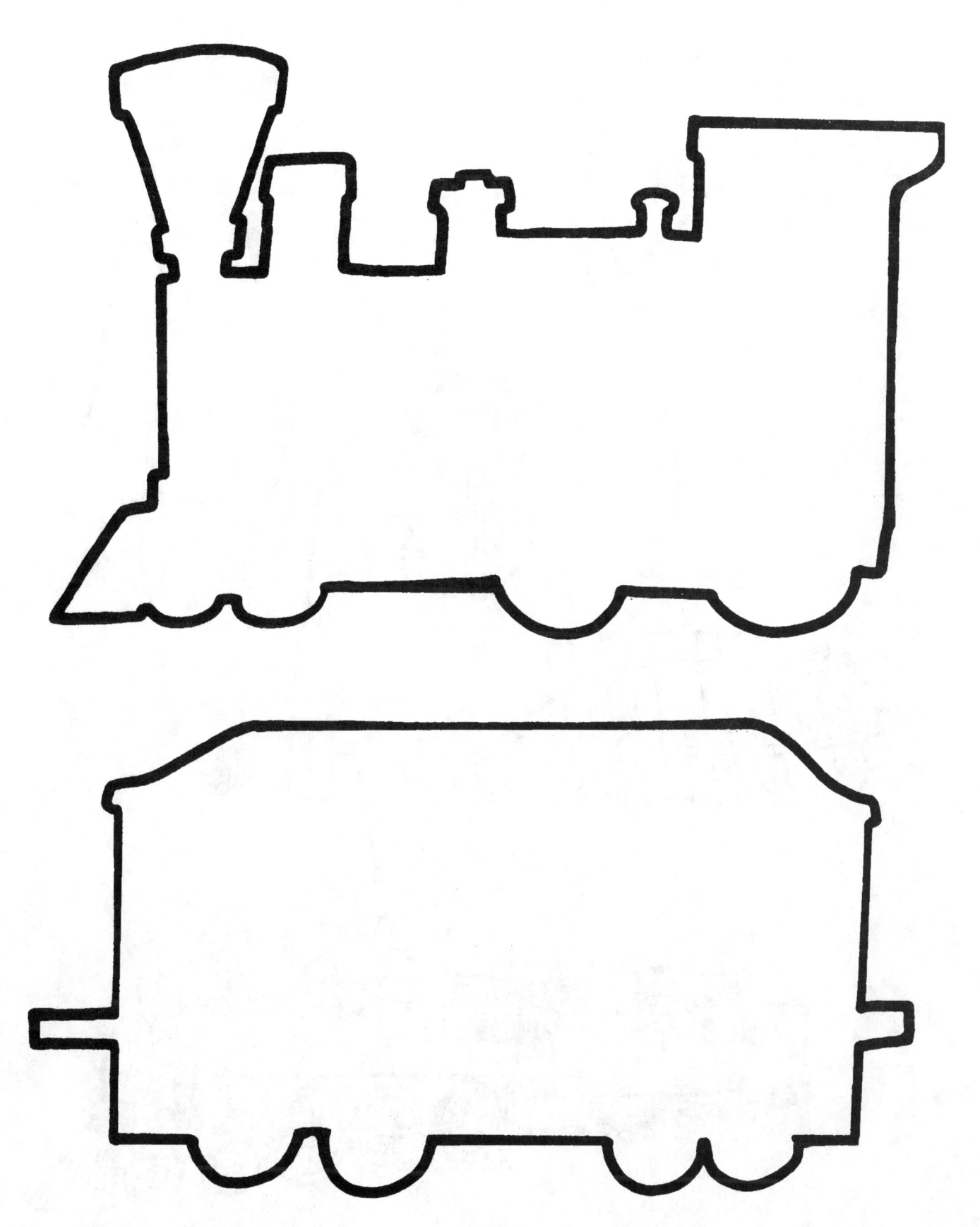

©1995 Teacher Created Materials, Inc. 77 #868 May Monthly Activities—Early Childhood

Trains *Patterns*

Clip Art and Patterns *(cont.)*

#868 May Monthly Activities—Early Childhood 78 ©1995 Teacher Created Materials, Inc.

Trains   Rewards

Bookmarks and Badges

I know the color black.

I know the letter T

Have students color the engine black and wear their badges home.

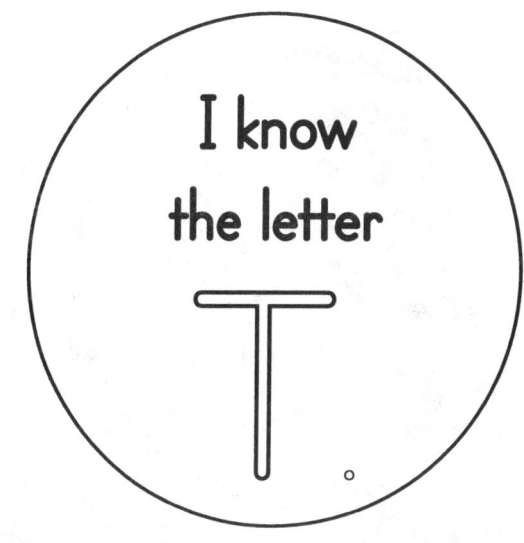

Have students color their badges and wear them home.

I know I can!

Let's read about trains.

Here comes the Reading Express!

Read *The Little Engine That Could* by Watty Piper (Platt and Munk, 1976) with the class. Then, let each student color a badge and wear it home.

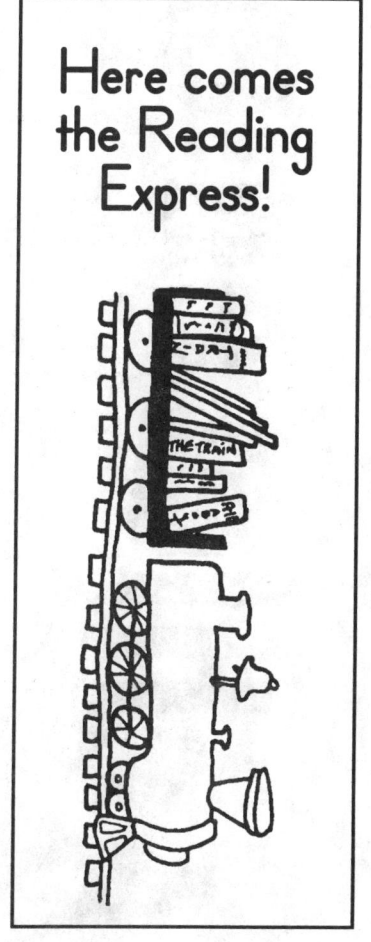

Although most early childhood students have not yet learned to read, they enjoy having bookmarks to use while reading with their families at home.

©1995 Teacher Created Materials, Inc.   79   #868 May Monthly Activities—Early Childhood

Trains   Award

Achievement Award

_____ has earned our

Classroom Achievement Award

for

BEING A GOOD FRIEND:

_____
Teacher's Signature

_____
Date

#868 May Monthly Activities—Early Childhood   80   ©1995 Teacher Created Materials, Inc.